Girls in Khaki

Girls in Khaki

A HISTORY OF THE ATS IN THE SECOND WORLD WAR

BARBARA GREEN

First published 2012

The History Press
The Mill, Brimscombe Port
Stroud, Gloucestershire, GL5 2QG
www.thehistorypress.co.uk

Reprinted 2015

British Library Cataloguing in Publication Data.
A catalogue record for this book is available from the British Library.

ISBN 978 0 7524 6350 6

Typesetting and origination by The History Press
Printed in Great Britain

Contents

Acknowledgements

My thanks go to all the ATS veterans who contributed so generously to this book with accounts of their wartime service, and to the WRAC Association Area and Branch secretaries who passed around word of the project.

I would also like to thank the following people who helped me in various ways on behalf of the organisations that they represent: Emma Lefley at the Picture Library, National Army Museum and Kate Swann and the team at the Templer Study Centre, National Army Museum who were both so helpful. Simon McCormack (House and Collections Manager) at the National Trust, Kedleston Hall for allowing me to quote from the National Trust book, *Secrets and Soldiers*, and Denise Young for help in obtaining the book. Jonathan Byrne, Roll of Honour Administrator at the Bletchley Park Trust for his advice and permission to quote from the Roll. Kerry Johnson and John Gallehawk for allowing me to quote from their book *Figuring it out at Bletchley Park 1939–1945*. Bianca Taubert of the Adjutant General's Corps Museum for her help in obtaining ATS photos and searching out information about RAEC Formation Colleges. Steve Rogers of the War Graves Photographic Project for his advice and photographs of Heverlee Cemetery. Susan Sopala of Mostyn Estates Ltd, Llandudno. Captain S.C. Fenwick RE for all the information he provided about the HPC and especially for allowing me to see *Postmen at War* – an unpublished history of the Army Postal Services from the Middle Ages to 1945 by Colonel E.T. Vallance CBE ERD (late RE). *The Daily Telegraph* for permission to quote from obituaries. Imperial War Museum Research Room for providing copies of two ATS War Office pamphlets.

To all those who are not mentioned, but were equally generous with their support and encouragement – thank you.

Introduction

George R.I.

WHEREAS WE deem it expedient to provide an organization whereby certain non-combatant duties in connection with Our Military and Air Forces may from time to time be performed by women: OUR WILL AND PLEASURE is that there shall be formed an organization to be designated the Auxiliary Territorial Service. OUR FURTHER WILL AND PLEASURE is that women shall be enrolled in the Service under such conditions and subject to such qualifications as may be laid down by Our Army Council from time to time.

Given at Our Court of St. James's this 9th day of September, 1938, in the 2nd year of Our Reign.

By His Majesty's Command
LESLIE HORE-BELISHA

So there it was. The Royal Warrant that formally established the (Women's) Auxiliary Territorial Service in 1938 as Britain faced the threat of war with Germany.

This is the story of those remarkable women who carried out duties, long thought to be beyond their feminine capabilities, with courage and determination. ATS girls grasped their new-found opportunities for further education, higher wages, skilled employment, management roles, and for a different future from the housebound duties of their mother and the low-paid domestic jobs that were abundant in earlier times.

Many common themes run through accounts of the wartime experiences that ex-ATS girls, or their families, relate in this book.

Training camps were set up all over the country; some recruits did their initial basic training within their home area, but others travelled long distances to areas that were unknown even to their parents. Many families had often visited only the nearest seaside resort for their annual holiday; to go from the south-east to the north of England, or from England to Scotland did come as a bit of a shock for some.

Historic houses and estates, many still owned by the original aristocratic families, were requisitioned or bought by the British government at the outbreak of war. They provided a common feature of service life. In fact, it's not unusual to read accounts by ATS girls that mention 'numerous huts built in the grounds to house military personnel'. Bletchley Park, which today has become one of the more famous locations, actually built its secretive structure around hut numbers only, without any description of what was going on inside them.

The most famous hut of all was probably the eponymous Nissen hut. ATS comments about these structures centre around the problems of keeping the coal-fired 'central heating' stove alight in the middle of the hut on a very meagre ration of coal – usually one bucket per day, not to be used until late afternoon– and around the initiative shown by the girls in obtaining additional supplies. Actually these huts were not just a feature of life in the army of the Second World War; their existence stretched for decades on either side of it. They had been designed in 1916 to house troops and were in use at least until the sixties. They were what we would now call a 'flat-pack' – but pre-fabricated from corrugated steel, with distinct curved walls. The hut could be adapted for use as accommodation, offices, storage or, occasionally, as a church. The next size up in the hut hierarchy was the Romney, which might be used for depot or unit storage, cookhouses and canteens or recreation rooms like those provided for ATS companies.

Ex-ATS members who describe themselves as having come from quiet, sheltered backgrounds could find the chaos and noise of their training camp disturbing. Strange uniforms, strange rules and regulations, so many other girls from so many different backgrounds, strange drill routines on a barrack square. Familiar feelings shared by anyone who has taken that first step out on to the drill square under the beady eye of a company sergeant major (CSM); or struggled to get uniform kit laid out on a bed to the exact spacing specified by higher authority; or ironed a uniform shirt to the required standard, which was especially difficult during summer months when jackets could be discarded and 'shirt-sleeve order' was permitted. To the uninitiated recruit this often translated as just 'rolling shirt sleeves up above the elbow'. Not quite! The measurement above the elbow had to be exact, as had the depth of the resultant 'cuff' before the creases were pressed in.

One happier theme of the times was dancing. Wherever male units were located, nearby ATS groups would be invited to the dances that they arranged – in canteens, drill halls, civilian dance halls in a neighbouring town. ATS veterans remember going to dances, which offered an escape from hard and often dirty jobs, relaxation, entertainment and, not least, potential romance.

Another happy theme was the friendships that formed between girls sharing service life – the trials and tribulations, the jokes, the frustrations, the characters and antics of officers and senior NCOs. The girls enjoyed especially the off-duty gatherings for chats about possible postings, the different lives and boyfriends left behind, civilian jobs, family attitudes to their new life in uniform. Many of those friendships have survived into the twenty-first century and are probably familiar to all who have worn uniform, regardless of time and place. As one ATS veteran put it, 'The comradeship was wonderful'.

A common experience for many ATS girls, especially those who were billeted in private houses or in properties that had been requisitioned for them in towns and villages, was the kindness of civilians. Despite all the shortages, there might be shared meals, or tea and sandwiches, even surprise birthday cakes. ATS members who volunteered for overseas service after D-Day also found friendship and generosity amongst the people of Belgium and Holland, even from those who had been left with virtually nothing themselves.

A comment that emerges only in hindsight (and perhaps with the aid of rose-tinted spectacles) is 'I wish I'd stayed in after the war ended'. Service life was uncertain for women in 1946. There were so many men expecting to return, either in uniform or as civilians, to their old jobs, many of which had been done by the ATS during the war. Of course, many women left the service to set up home with men whom they'd married during the war, others to marry fiancés who were themselves being demobbed. Some just wanted to return to civilian life and jobs. A minority then missed service life so much that they re-enlisted.

Finally there is one rather trivial theme that deserves a mention – the supplies of hot tea that everybody remembers because they kept them going, especially when so many duties meant suffering from the cold or tiredness or both. Whether out of giant metal teapots or stainless steel buckets, drunk from mugs or jam jars or the best china in the homes of kind civilians – they seem to have a special place in the hearts of ATS girls.

It must never be forgotten, however, that while the ATS girls in khaki now recall memories of hard work and friendship, danger and laughter, they

The 'common theme' of tea. The girls partake in tea from a lovely pot and small tea cups out in a garden or rural area. Eileen Sharp (née Horobin) is on the extreme left. Courtesy of P. Sharp.

shared with the rest of the population at home that fear of the arrival of the telegram telling them that they were never again to see their father, brother, fiancé, husband or sister.

Elsie Roberts (née Guinan) knew all about that. She was an ATS Ack-Ack (anti-aircraft) height-finder with 593 and 478 (M) HAA Batteries – and on duty at her command post when somebody relayed the message that her brother, a Royal Marine Commando, had been killed.

The skill and dedication of so many ATS members during the Second World War defined the future of women in army uniform. Despite the fact that the achievements of the ATS forestalled any return to pre-war attitudes about the place of women in the services, there was uncertainty about how their future structure should be organised.

To cover the period at the end of the war ATS members who wanted to remain in uniform were granted 'extended service' terms.

Discussions started about the incorporation of the service into the British Army as a regular corps. Yet it still took three years of hard bargaining before the plans were enacted. At last, on 1 February 1949, the Women's Royal Army Corps took over from the ATS, whose remaining members were attested into the new corps. Different badges for sure, but they still wore khaki with pride.

One

Organisation

The history of the Auxiliary Territorial Service – the ATS – really began in the middle of the First World War.

As early as 1916, in the face of heavy casualties on the French battle-fields, the British government was forced to acknowledge that women were needed in the army to take over non-combatant roles from soldiers, who could then be released for front-line duties.

Consequently, in early 1917, a new voluntary service was formed – the Women's Army Auxiliary Corps (WAAC). The corps received Royal Patronage in 1918, becoming Queen Mary's Army Auxiliary Corps (QMAAC). The precedent was set.

Mrs Mona Chalmers Watson was appointed as head of the corps. Helen Gwynne-Vaughan was appointed Chief Controller WAAC (Overseas), responsible for the organisation and running of the corps' operations in France and Belgium. She left for France on 19 March 1917. Twenty-one years later, as Dame Helen, she became the first Director of the ATS.

So who was this woman who twice took a lead in the establishment of a women's section of the British Army?

Helen Gwynne-Vaughan GBE LLD DSc

First and foremost she was a Victorian, born as Helen Charlotte Isabella Fisher in 1879. This makes her achievements and her career even more remarkable, given the general status of women in the nineteenth and early twentieth century, when those who had the ability and the courage to do so struggled in all walks of life to achieve their potential and their ambitions.

To the horror of her parents, she took a science degree at King's College London – a BSc in Botany. By 1909, she was head of the Department of Botany at Birkbeck College, London. After the war she was appointed Professor of Botany at London University, when Birkbeck College became part of that university. In 1911 she had married a fellow botanist, David Gwynne-Vaughan, who died in 1915.

The full story of Dame Helen's many activities during the years leading up to the formation of the WAAC in 1917 is told in her autobiography *Service with the Army*, published in 1944.

Helen Gwynne-Vaughan's work overseas in the QMAAC was so highly thought of that, in 1918, she was asked to become Commandant of the Women's Royal Air Force to carry out a thorough restructuring of that organisation. She continued in this appointment until December 1919, when the demobilisation of the WRAF was almost complete. The QMAAC was disbanded in 1921.

Her work during these years brought the award of DBE in 1919, enhanced in the twenties to GBE (Dame Grand Cross of the Order of the British Empire).

The Inter-War Years

Dame Helen returned to academia, concentrating on research in mycology, the branch of botany that specialises in the study of fungi. In 1922 Cambridge University Press published her book on this topic, the title of which has arguably only one word in it – fungi – that is either pronounceable or comprehensible for the lay reader. Interestingly, this is more than just an odd historical fact about Dame Helen's career. In 2010 the Cambridge Library Collection (Life Sciences) republished this book for researchers and professionals as part of their scheme for reviving books of 'enduring scholarly value'. Even in the twenty-first century she is still remembered as 'an influential mycologist', in which capacity she had been elected President of the British Mycological Society. Although she died in 1967, it is therefore possible to think of Dame Helen's work as spanning three centuries.

Despite the demands of her academic career during the inter-war years, Dame Helen still found time to get involved with the Girl Guide movement at the request of Lady Baden-Powell. She progressed from the executive council to the vice-chairmanship in 1925 under Lord Baden-Powell and then to chairman in 1928. During her earlier career she had always set great store by the value of training and considered the systems of training and voluntary discipline in the Girl Guides to be 'splendid'.

Dame Helen was also a woman who, in her own words, was 'convinced that, in any future major war, women would sooner or later be employed with His Majesty's Forces'. Her professorial status didn't diminish her interest in military matters and strategy. In 1924 she became the Territorial Army Association's representative on the Voluntary Aid Detachment Council and was also, until 1938, the chairman of the mobilisation committee. In addition she served on various departmental committees, unrelated to military matters but giving her varied and useful experience.

Discussions had been taking place since 1920 about the role of women in wartime and the need for some kind of peacetime corps of women who would be trained and ready to serve with defined ranks and military status. Progress was slow and decisions were delayed, partly through lack of funding for any new organisation. An anti-women attitude amongst all ranks of the male army probably played its part as well. Dame Helen kept in touch with discussions and developments at the War Office in relation to the employment of women in emergencies. From 1934 onwards such discussions began to take on a more formal character. As the threat of war grew ever more serious, plans for the formation of a single female corps intensified; she, however, had always argued strongly that each of the three services (army, air force, navy) should have their own women's section, subject to military discipline.

Although the ATS was brought into existence by Royal Warrant on 9 September 1938, it was the evening of 27 September before this was made public in a broadcast by the BBC. Following a tradition of Royal Patronage, HRH Princess Mary, the Princess Royal, then accepted the position of Controller ATS in Yorkshire. In 1941 she officially became Controller Commandant ATS. Her subsequent interest in the ATS and its role within the British Army, together with her visits to ATS companies, did much to raise morale and establish the value of the service. Royalty was held in high regard at this time. Queen Elizabeth (later, the Queen Mother) was Commandant-in-Chief of the ATS from 1940 until 1949.

As the first Director of the ATS Dame Helen must have felt a degree of satisfaction in both having prophesied a formal role in the armed forces for women in any future major war and being selected, probably after some political lobbying and intrigue, to lead the female side of the army.

Helen Gwynne-Vaughan inspecting ATS at Manorbier. Illustrates her looking 'dowdy' in her uniform and the ATS in the blue blazers and white skirts that they wore when attached to some RA units. Courtesy of the National Army Museum.

In her new role she was variously described as intelligent, formidable, intellectually sharp, severe, tactless, thrusting, overbearing, dowdy and an outstanding organiser who couldn't tolerate fools gladly and made juniors very nervous. Later Dame Leslie Whateley, who became the third Director of the ATS, sought to mitigate this harsh opinion of Dame Helen after working on her staff. Dame Leslie attributed to her predecessor the foundations upon which the ATS was built over subsequent years.

Yet Dame Helen's own experiences had taught her that leading the ATS wasn't going to be easy; she'd been exposed during the First World War, and afterwards, to the way in which many traditional males viewed any competent and determined women who wanted to invade their select circles. Indeed it wasn't overwhelming admiration of female qualities that was the prime reason for the establishment of the women's services and the eventual introduction of female conscription during the Second World War; and it certainly wasn't any push from the then unknown 'equality' lobby. It was simply the need to release ever greater numbers of fighting troops for the front line amidst the continuing shortage of manpower.

Britain wasn't the only country to recognise this requirement. Russia had to relinquish its traditional objection to women serving in the army because of the heavy losses suffered by its Red Army after the German invasion of 1941, known as Operation Barbarossa. American senior commanders had also had similar doubts about women serving in the armed forces, but any opposition was eventually overridden by General Eisenhower.

In addition to outside opposition to the idea of women in the armed services, Dame Helen was also aware that her age, and perhaps her old-fashioned views, might exacerbate existing difficulties. After all, she was 60 when the ATS was formed and at that time, although not today, that would be considered to be a fairly advanced age.

Subsequently she admitted that 'the ATS got off to a bad start'. This view was confirmed by the Princess Royal in her capacity as Controller Commandant of the ATS. She wrote a preface to *As Thoughts Survive*, a personal account of the ATS in wartime by its third director, Dame Leslie Whateley. In HRH Princess Mary's own words, 'The ATS started with many disadvantages of inexperience, but with the great advantage of enthusiasm. From out of this there grew a solid regimental discipline and true military adaptability.'

In Dame Helen's view the bad start could be attributed largely to the inadequate selection and training of the first officers; many were unsuited to the task of leadership and, conversely, those who might have been were fully occupied elsewhere. Early problems in general were often euphemistically described as 'teething troubles'; but what did that mean?

The first factor that led to initial confusion was the existence of three women's organisations involved in army functions in the thirties.

These were as follows. The Women's Legion, a new successor to the Women's Legion of the First World War. That original, private society had been formed by Lady Londonderry to provide cooks for army cookhouses that lacked sufficient staff. The girls were all volunteers but the Army Council did pay for those it hired through the Legion. It continued in existence into the thirties, by which time it had a Mechanical Transport Section. In 1934 Lady Londonderry was asked to set up a new organisation for women who might be trained in some way that would prove useful in any future emergency. She became president of this, assisted by Dame Helen as chairman, but, confusingly, they kept the title of Women's Legion. After much discussion they decided to concentrate on anti-gas training (which only lasted for a couple of years) and officer training.

In 1936, for various reasons this 'new' Women's Legion was disbanded. The original Legion, still in existence, provided a Motor Transport Section.

The Emergency Service: this took over the work of training female officers under Dame Helen's leadership. She had already set up a training school in Regent's Park Barracks in London. Subsequently she was made responsible for setting up a more formal School of Instruction for Officers at the Duke of York's headquarters in Chelsea.

The Women's Transport Service – the FANY (First Aid Nursing Yeomanry): this service had been in existence since 1909 when its original purpose had been for female horse-riders to enter war zones to rescue and treat wounded soldiers. Horse riding was naturally superseded by vehicle driving so that by 1938 the FANY's main role lay in producing motor driver companies.

Originally these three services were to form the basis of a joint army service that would be called the Women's Auxiliary Defence Service – a title that changed on the realisation that WADS would not be a suitable acronym! The search for a title for the new women's service proved to be difficult – either because the title could be abbreviated in an unsuitable way, such as WADS, or because the acronym was already in use if the 'W' was removed, leaving something like ADS – the Army Dental Service. It seemed to be a feature of military bureaucracy that whenever any new organisation was planned there would be arguments about names, titles and allocation of ranks before its actual purpose was defined. 'Auxiliary Territorial Service' eventually emerged as the chosen option. Unfortunately and unlike the other two women's services, the omission of the 'Women' still led to some initial confusion; but as the war progressed 'ATS' became well known because of the contribution that its girls made to the war effort.

The second factor that led to problems, although it was thought initially to be the best option, was that the ATS was established as part of the Territorial Army (TA). This meant that it was organised, like the TA itself, on a county basis. Right from the start this caused chaos when women, hearing the calls for ATS volunteers, turned up as requested at their local TA headquarters or drill hall demanding to be enrolled. Some TA officers hadn't even been warned about this possibility and didn't know what to do with their new recruits. Sometimes they were told to turn up for only a couple of hours a week for basic training and to carry out secretarial and clerical duties. Disillusioned, many left at that point because they were volunteers and free to do so – exactly why Helen Gwynne-Vaughan wanted ATS recruits to be enlisted on a more formal basis.

Then there were the problems, already mentioned, with the appointment of officers. Helen Gwynne-Vaughan had always believed strongly in the need for leadership training for officers, that was why she had organised it in the Emergency Service. So what was the difficulty in the early months of the ATS? Again it related to the link with the TA. When they realised that there was a need for ATS officers they thought that the easiest source would lie in the county structure of titled ladies and wives of local dignitaries and landowners who, with many other ladies, were well known in the county for their voluntary and charitable work. In the TA's predecessors – the Militia and the Yeomanry – this had been the method of appointing male officers for as long as those military formations had existed but this solution obviously had pros and cons for the ATS. None of the above criteria could guarantee leadership potential or any of the other qualities required for officers. So there was justifiable criticism of the competency and efficiency, or lack of it, amongst the officer community of the ATS. As one ATS veteran described it, 'They were useless and only got an immediate commission because they were society girls'. However, there were many officers who quite rightly felt that generalisations like this were grossly unfair. Such comments were resented by the leaders of platoons and units that were well organised, active, smart and gave a good impression of the service in front of the general public. These officers probably had some kind of previous experience that could be developed into leadership with more specific training.

As the number of ATS recruits grew rapidly from the initial 17,000, the question of officer competency had to be tackled officially. Those who were plainly unsuited for the positions were discharged as quickly as possible, thereby making room for efficient junior ranks to be promoted; this also had a beneficial effect on morale. Confidential reports were instituted for all officer ranks. The number of ATS Officer Cadet Training Units (OCTU) was expanded to provide the hundreds of officers, both technical and regimental, who were needed. Reactions to the subject of 'officers' vary. Many ATS weren't interested in the squabbles and politics of higher command; for them the most important event involving a senior officer would be a visit by the current director, especially if she was accompanied by royalty. Their platoon or unit officer would have the most influence in their day-to-day lives. Most of them were 'quite nice' or 'very helpful'; but one obviously failed the test – after more than sixty years she was remembered by an ATS veteran as simply 'a bitch'!

Equally important was the training of NCOs; one aspect of a first promotion to the single stripe of a lance corporal was how to cope with the move from being one of the crowd to having some authority, albeit slight, over that crowd, without alienating anyone. Another reason for the urgent need to recruit and train officers and senior NCOs was to enable the hundreds of ATS recruits to be trained by female instructors rather than by men.

On top of all the practical problems of organisation, administration and training there was the relationship between the long-established FANY and the newly formed ATS. This, inevitably, proved to be a very difficult situation, not helped by the deep personal animosity between the leaders of the two organisations. Mary Baxter-Ellis, Commandant of the FANY, and Helen Gwynne-Vaughan were both veterans of the First World War but despite that, or perhaps because of it, they now appeared to be sworn enemies.

In addition, members of the FANY thought themselves to be far superior to those girls who were joining the ATS. They wanted to remain independent of the ATS and continue to run their units as they always had done. Indeed, for a while they did do this while the ATS was trying to sort out its own problems. The FANY, with all its experience of motor transport, was training drivers within its own organisation virtually independently of the ATS. As if this wasn't bad enough, the ATS was run according to military tradition and regulations, which meant a strict division between officers and 'other ranks'; the FANY had no such restrictions, which absolutely infuriated Dame Helen. She brought certain beliefs with her into the new era but she had to fight hard for her ideas. She wanted enlistment for her women, not enrolment as volunteers. (This was one of the few areas in which she had the support of Miss Baxter Ellis of the FANY.) She also wanted payment, which she saw as an essential element of being able to impose discipline on those who were simply volunteers. It's not too difficult to imagine all the squabbling that took place, even while the country remained under the threat of war.

When the FANY realised that they were not to remain as an independent body within the ATS they raised the issue of whether or not they would still wear the FANY flash on their ATS uniforms. Resentments and disputes were silenced when the newly formed ATS was recognised formally as the women's service of the regular army, and the FANY were officially incorporated into it. Further progress in the status of the ATS followed the demands of the country as the war continued. On 10 April 1941 the Secretary of State for War announced that the ATS, in view of their achievements so far and due to the need to increase their numbers, would be given full military status. This meant that the service would be subject to military discipline and required to extend its roles even further to meet the army's needs. Adjustments would be made in the application of the regulations of the Army Act to the service – for example, ATS members would not be required to fight and, although they would be subject to a court martial for certain offences (as were the men), the system would ensure that a female officer would be available to assist in the disciplinary procedures.

There were quite a few changes at this time which met with approval; the rank structure was brought into line with that of the male army introducing, for example, the rank of Warrant Officer Class 1 and 2 and pay for trade qualifications; officers were commissioned – i.e. they now held the King's Commission.

The next demand made by the government on the female population was that of conscription in December 1941 because of the continuing shortage of manpower. Some groups of women and some professions were exempt of course. Mothers with small children or responsibility for the care of elderly relatives, and teachers were examples of the exempt groups. Others had the choice of doing factory work and other essential civilian jobs, as 'directed' by the authorities, or joining one of the services.

Directors of the ATS (DATS)

Helen Gwynne-Vaughan was asked to retire in July 1941. Although she was not in a position to object she accepted the decision with outward equanimity, particularly in the light of what she saw as her achievements since 1938. And these achievements were recognised by many senior officers – even those who didn't always see eye to eye with her.

There was certainly a need to improve the image of the service in the eyes of the public and the press. This needed somebody who was competent but younger, preferably an officer who was attractive and could show off a smart uniform to advantage. Although such qualities would not normally be the exclusive basis for a senior appointment the authorities had recognised an urgent need for image-building in view of the adverse publicity the ATS had attracted.

This new role fell to the then Senior Commander Jean Knox (the equivalent rank of major in the army). She was in her early thirties, attractive and wore her uniform well – partly because she had made small changes to the design. The most obvious of these was that she had the skirts shortened – still below the knee but not the mid-calf length of the earlier pattern.

The service jacket was also given a full belt at the waist and slimmer breast pockets. So the public image of the ATS improved, but Jean Knox resigned after two years on health grounds.

Senior Controller Leslie Whateley was Jean Knox's deputy for the two years of her appointment as DATS. The two officers shared the opinion that the image of the ATS had to be improved. Leslie Whateley, although she had recognised some of the worthy qualities of Helen Gwynne-Vaughan, believed that one of her failings was that she viewed the female members of the ATS as just another version of the male soldier. Although as few as possible concessions were made to their femininity, Leslie Whateley and her senior officers did recognise that some allowances should be made wherever possible, especially in 'comfort' areas like accommodation and ablutions. Needless to say, there are plenty of examples where this good intention failed! Nevertheless, the relationship between Jean Knox and her deputy had worked out well.

Leslie Whateley's move to the top as DATS in October 1943 went smoothly. She had already dealt with, and taken responsibility for, most areas of administration at the War Office while Jean Knox was away inspecting ATS units and the conditions under which they operated. She obviously valued her association with the higher echelons of civilian and military society and, in her own words, did a lot of 'dining with'; but it must have smoothed her path as she toured the country, attended parades and visited overseas locations in the Middle East, Italy, Athens, Cyprus, Greece, Nairobi.

Leslie Whateley faced a difficult situation in what turned out to be the closing months of the war. In December 1944 the government decided that overseas postings for the ATS would become compulsory, which caused an outcry. Then, as DATS, Chief Controller Whateley obtained permission (and supplies) to write a 'personal' letter to every member of the ATS commenting on the situation, the reasons for it and the exemptions that would apply to this new regulation. She explained that although there had been hundreds of volunteers for overseas duty it was a question of whether the qualifications and trades of those volunteers matched the overseas vacancies. Her second explanation covered that old topic, shortage of manpower in the army, especially in front-line infantry divisions. She gave various valid reasons but left out one or two causes of the perceived need for more ATS to take over duties from male troops. Although it seemed obvious by then that the Allies were going to defeat Germany, there was a lingering question mark over whether or not there would be some kind of final push

Leslie Whateley (DATS). Courtesy of the Adjutant General's Corps Museum.

by the German forces. The British military, from a political point of view, also wanted to have enough strong infantry units to hold their own in the agreed division of Germany between the Allies; and even if victory came soon in Western Europe plans had to be drawn up to reinforce army units in South-East Asia. There war against Japan continued and might well have done so for a couple more years, with increasing losses of Allied manpower.

Dame Leslie, as she was by the time of her retirement in 1946, had been giving some thought to her successor. Although there would be three nominations she herself had decided that the best candidate was Mary Tyrwhitt. Mary had organised training courses in the ATS, including those for officers and this in itself was a valuable experience. She then served as Leslie Whateley's deputy, giving the DATS an opportunity to pass over to her a lot of responsibility during her absences. Mary Tyrwhitt had been born in the early part of the century, putting her in her mid-forties at the time of the handover; this gave her the degree of maturity that would be needed to carry on the ATS and negotiate its future now that the war was over.

She subsequently projected the image of a new, more modern women's army, when she took the ATS through a reorganisation into the Women's Royal Army Corps (WRAC) in 1949 – a regular corps of the British Army.

Brigadier Mary Tyrwhitt.
Courtesy of the Adjutant
General's Corps Museum.

Two

Recruitment and Basic Training

There were all kinds of ways in which the authorities encouraged women to join the ATS – radio broadcasts; recruiting parades carried out in town centres by girls who had already been through basic training with extra instruction in marching; posters; press; and magazine articles.

Anne Scott-James, a journalist and later radio personality, was the women's editor of the *Picture Post* during the war. She ran a series of features exploring the way in which women's lives were being changed by the war. A reporter was sent to accompany a group of ATS recruits to record their experiences.

These all had some effect on recruiting, but girls had many of their own reasons for joining the ATS:

- ♦ family members might already be serving; friends or relatives might already have been killed in action, creating the view that 'it was time to do my bit'
- ♦ meeting old school friends who were home on leave and telling tales of their new life
- ♦ girls might want to get away from domestic work, especially if they were in low-paid jobs; or they might be tired of helping out their mothers in large families as unpaid workers; or they might be members of better-off families who had lost their maids and other staff to war work of whatever kind, which was probably better paid. Daughters were then expected to step in and fill the gaps, but were not keen on this

- for adventure
- and last, but probably not least, it might have been sheer contrariness in the face of family opposition

Getting Kitted Out

The main problem that the first ATS volunteers had with uniforms was actually getting them – or at least getting a complete set issued at the same time. That's not surprising given that the initial intake for the ATS was expected to be 17,000. Many just built up their kit as the various items arrived.

The basic issue of kit consisted of underwear and khaki stockings (khaki knickers always being referred to as 'passion killers'), two pairs of shoes, plimsolls, a tunic (jacket) with two skirts, three shirts (with detached collars), ties, a pullover, towels and, with a bit of luck, something to keep out the wet and the cold like a greatcoat. Special trades also needed extras like slacks, boots and thick socks, overalls and gloves. Some got more, some less.

Two essential items on the list were:

- the 'Housewife' – a small sewing kit for emergency repairs
- the 'button stick'. This gadget was a flat metal device that had a slit up the middle so that it could be slid around buttons to prevent the brass cleaner getting on to the cloth of the uniform jacket during cleaning. There were no 'stay-brite' buttons in those days

One figure of male authority claimed that 'the uniforms are skillfully graded to the vagaries of the feminine figure'. It's possible that with an eventual intake of more than 200,000 women, not every recruit would agree with that claim, but matters slowly improved especially after the early intakes; and certainly after Jean Knox, when she took over as director, made some changes. Probably the most skilful grading of all was done by the ATS girls themselves – to their uniform caps.

Did Dame Helen Gwynne-Vaughan have her sharp, authoritarian tongue in her cheek when she reported somewhat drily in her *Service in the Army* that she had received a letter from one of the TA branches at the War Office anxiously enquiring about ATS undergarments? Probably not, because she had already considered the matter herself and consulted old Comrades Associations of which she was a member. What to do about these ATS 'under-garments'. Should they be issued as part of the regulation kit or should women receive an allowance to buy their own supply? It was agreed

Two unnamed girls 'modelling' their passion killers. Courtesy of Esther Pring.

by all concerned that these garments should be authorised and issued as standard to everyone. This meant that there would be no difference in what was worn by any ATS recruit.

A second worry was that ordnance officers were unaccustomed to dealing with feminine underwear in military store houses. There was concern that they might not be happy with this new experience even though any undue embarrassment might be quelled by the sight of the ATS 'passion killers'. The most tactful response to that was to point out that they would be relieved of any discomfort by the opening of a separate section at the RAOC clothing depot at COD Branston, run by and for the ATS.

It's easy to list 'shoes' as just another item of kit; it's only when they turn out to be flat, fairly heavy lace-ups that the contrast with some civilian lightweight shoes or high heels becomes apparent, causing blisters during the first few days of square-bashing with a drill instructor. Joan De-Vall, who served with the Royal Artillery (RA), remembers the effect of drilling in heavy footwear after her civilian winkle-pickers and high heels. She and her colleagues resorted to bowls of warm water and mauve potash.

Appearance

There was usually at least one member of a squad or unit who couldn't persuade her hair to stay neatly under her cap, or whose skirt or trouser hem caught on something and unravelled, or who had one item of uniform that resisted the ministrations of an iron; but it was generally accepted that after a few weeks of basic training, with its emphasis on drill, polishing, inspections and pressing, the ATS would look and feel smart.

So what about make-up and cosmetics? Reactions varied. Some girls, especially the younger ones, thought that they had enough to do during their hours on duty without worrying about make-up; with clear skin an application of cold cream would suffice. It might be different for dances and dates. Interestingly, in women's magazines of the period, the adverts from the established cosmetic manufacturers like Yardley and Elizabeth Arden often used an outline sketch of a woman's face with some form of peaked cap above it – the detail of a badge was blurred but obviously signified a girl in service uniform. The message seemed to be that doing men's hard, urgent, dirty work, in or out of doors, for long hours was no excuse for ignoring personal grooming and freshness. Looking one's best was a way of keeping morale up. That was true, but keeping to a 'beauty regime', as recommended by one manufacturer, would perhaps be a regime too far for the ATS; although in this, as in so many areas of their new life, girls in khaki didn't lack initiative. Those who were likely to be called out during night-time emergencies usually recount how they always kept their 'dinky' curlers in under their helmets – and how they were courageous enough to ignore totally the ensuing comments of their male colleagues.

Badges Uniforms and Medals

Badges
<u>Figure 1</u>
Illustrates the brass ATS cap badge. Although these two images are of the same issue badge there are very slight differences between them. This demonstrates that they have been produced by different manufacturers, each using a different die to stamp out the badges.

Such a slight variation is similar to that present in the production of khaki uniform items; the labels in the uniforms illustrate the many civilian sources from which they came as they always include the manufacturer's name.

Figure 2
The ATS brass shoulder title worn on the epaulette of the service dress tunic.

Figure 3
A very small version of the standard brass ATS badge, perhaps used as a tie-pin or a sweetheart brooch.

Figure 4
An officer's bronze cap badge.

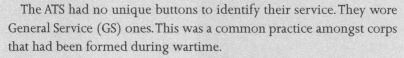

By 1942 the brass badges and buttons were being replaced by plastic ones as an economy measure.

The ATS had no unique buttons to identify their service. They wore General Service (GS) ones. This was a common practice amongst corps that had been formed during wartime.

Uniforms

Bearing in mind that ATS girls had a song to cover every eventuality, here is one to explain attitudes to uniform:

Thanks for the memories
Of the day we went to war
In Army haute couture

A uniform and underwear
Of the kind our Mothers wore.

Small changes were made to ATS uniforms over the wartime years. Although hardly a 'design modification', probably the most obvious and flattering change was that of shortening the length of the skirt. This had been introduced by Chief Controller Jean Knox when she became Director ATS in 1941. Tunic pockets were altered to make them less bulky and a belt was added to the tunic. Despite Jean Knox's intention to smarten up the ATS, most of the changes were not specified in the interests of female fashion but to economise on material. Greatcoats, service dress tunics and battledress blouses usually buttoned in the male style – left over right.

The ATS colours were dark brown, beech brown and green. They formed the ATS lanyard and the later cloth shoulder titles that replaced the brass ones. ATS Auxiliaries with Anti-Aircraft (AA) Command were permitted to wear the distinctive white lanyard of the Royal Artillery.

An additional item of ATS uniform that was not issued but had to be bought privately was the coloured field cap, in ATS colours. They were preferred by some when off duty or travelling home on leave, for example. Uniform had to be worn at all times and this optional extra relieved the drab khaki colour.

This photograph of Olive Kinghorn (née Helyer), whose ATS experiences are recounted in the 'Guns and Dancing' section of Chapter 3, demonstrates the attraction of the field cap compared with the regulation-issue cap.

Olive Kinghorn (née Helyer) on leave in 1943. Note field service cap. Courtesy of Olive Kingham.

Medals

The following are only general outline descriptions of the entitlement to wear certain medals. They are intended to give an overview of what serving ATS members may have been able to claim:

- 1939–1945 Star
  Awarded to personnel who completed six months' service in specified overseas operational areas
- 1940–1943 Africa Star
  There may have been some ATS who earned this Star for service in North Africa, particularly in rear-support echelons of the Eighth Army
- 1944–1945 France and Germany Star
  Awarded for operational service in France, Belgium, the Netherlands or Germany from 6 June 1944 to 8 May 1945. Earned by some ATS who volunteered for overseas posting to Western Europe after D-Day
- Defence Medal
  Awarded for those with three years' service at home
- War Medal 1939–1945
  Awarded to all full-time service personnel with at least twenty-eight days' service between 3 September 1939 and 2 September 1945

Basic Training

The majority of ATS veterans (like most soldiers and their fathers before them) can remember their basic training and many of the common reactions are described in the individual stories told later.

Perhaps the easiest introduction to army life was the experience of having arrived with a ticket at a local main railway station to find that there were a dozen or so other young women there bound for the same place. Time to chat, time to get to know one or two faces, time to discover that others had the same worries about their future.

Training camps, situated all round the country, provided the same initiation into army life. What would make a difference between them was the permanent staff. Some might be more pleasant than others, or have a greater tolerance of early mistakes. However, their primary role was, in one way or another, by the end of four weeks, to turn out a group of girls in khaki who were healthy, smart, disciplined and who understood military rules and regulations. Medicals included vaccinations that could make some girls feel unwell, checks for hair lice if that hadn't already been done in the barrack room by colleagues frightened of catching them, tests for pregnancy and venereal disease. We have to remember that with the male military personnel of all services VD was a constant worry, so medical staff were used to ensuring that it was kept under control. There was a lot of drill on the parade ground and marching as a squad between locations. Just in case that wasn't enough physical exercise for one day there would then be a Physical Training (PT) session, probably in the gym. There was instruction in the carrying and use of respirators (gas masks), with hated sessions of gas training which involved having to remove your respirator in an enclosed space that had been filled with gas – just for a few seconds so that you had an idea of what it would be like (apart from lethal) to be caught in a gas attack without protection. Usually a few gulps of fresh air repaired any temporary upset although some girls did suffer for some time afterwards.

There would always be a lecture on pay – how pay scales were structured according to rank and trade qualifications, which was of great interest. There was another pay topic that was particularly relevant to many recruits and that was how part of the weekly pay could be sent home to families who had become dependent partly on the wages being brought home from the civilian job that the recruit had previously had.

Much of the content of the basic training lectures would have come from 'Regulations for the ATS 1941'. Such pamphlets were common throughout the army; they covered anything and everything and were extremely detailed; the aim was obviously to ensure that no information was left out and no potential question left unanswered. Those entitled 'Regulations for' covered an individual regiment or corps; others included training manuals, running to several volumes on all kinds of weaponry – there was even one on the 'Training of War Dogs'.

So the 1941 ATS publication was a typical War Office pamphlet crammed with details – twelve sections covering organisation, documentation and records, discharge procedures, pay structure, discipline and courts martial, dress codes, medical matters, etc. Then there were fifteen appendices specifying the intricacies of pay rates, rank structure, trades and establishment figures. This latter appendix laid down, for example, how many officers and NCOs by rank and 'other ranks' were required for each military formation; then how many support personnel should be allocated to each size of formation, from cooks and orderlies to clerical staff, medics and drivers.

It was this attention to detail that explains why, for example, every ATS recruit got one of this and three of that included in their issue of uniform and accessories – all specified by higher authority. The depth of detail is highlighted by the fact that, while ATS recruits talked about going off to the cookhouse with their 'irons' – a knife, fork and spoon – the authorities identified thirty items to list under 'cutlery' in their 1941 Regulations.

In addition to six specialist roles for those employed in AA HAA batteries, there were thirty-six trades and occupations, from baker to wood-turner, available to recruits whose early predecessors had been considered simply as potential cooks, orderlies and clerks.

One section that would probably have been omitted from recruit lectures was the list of personal characteristics and qualities on which potential officers should be graded. Namely reliability, loyalty, experience, tact, powers of leadership, intelligence, firmness and manner.

Three

Alongside the Royal Artillery

The training and employment of ATS girls with the Royal Artillery (RA) owed its inception and continuing success to General Sir Frederick Pile, the General Officer Commanding-in-Chief of Anti-Aircraft (AA) Command throughout the war.

At various times during the war, but particularly in the first two years, his command suffered from acute manpower shortages. Eventually it became impossible to resolve this problem any longer by using earlier means. After discussing the matter with colleagues he came to the conclusion that women would be quite capable of meeting the manpower gaps in AA Command by serving in Mixed Batteries (MB). As General Pile said, 'There were many doubters in the early days but it proved a triumphant success.'

Training in MBs began in May 1941 and in August of that year the first one became operational. The girls carried out all the duties in a battery except those involving heavy manual labour and the actual firing of guns. The ratio of girls to men was two to one.

The general ordered that all Heavy Anti-Aircraft (HAA) batteries coming from training should be designated as mixed batteries, and, as more ATS girls came out of RA training, that existing HAA all-male batteries should be converted to MBs.

In 1942 a Royal Artillery officer – Major Rees Williams – wrote a brief article for *The Spectator* magazine entitled 'The Gunner Girls'. He reported that his colleagues, on learning that ATS girls were to be trained to work with

The *ATS/Ack-Ack Memorial at the National Arboretum at Alrewas, Staffordshire.* Courtesy of Lucy Bowyer.

Anti-Aircraft (AA) batteries, were 'at first incredulous and then inclined to scoff'. Some of General Pile's 'doubters' probably.

At an RA practice camp, where trainees fired at 'sleeves' trailed behind aircraft, Major Rees Williams saw the first ATS team to control firing at such a target. He wasn't critical but his comments were rather non-committal. A year later he was actually posted into a training regiment where the girls were working as part of a mixed battery. The ATS operated the instruments while the men fired the guns. Now he found the girls to be good at their job, well turned-out and smart on parade.

Still, he was probably an officer of the old school, although an honest one. He was not quite comfortable with the idea of regarding the girls as 'soldiers' – a concept that he found strange. As he explained it, 'soldiers of a special kind, of course, but soldiers fitting themselves to take a vital part in the defence of the country'. Finally he addressed one of the rumours that surrounded the ATS in the early days: 'The jibes one has heard about the behaviour of the ATS are so false as to be ludicrous. No mother need be afraid of entrusting her daughter to a gunner unit.'

Indeed, by the end of the war, General Pile's opinion was that 'The ATS, particularly in the Mixed Batteries, set a standard of bearing and conduct which in my opinion was not equalled by any other women's service'.

Experimental training for ATS girls who were destined for AA mixed batteries was undertaken. Their physical strength and technical capabilities were tested, as was their performance under firing conditions. The first German plane to be shot down by a mixed battery crashed in the Newcastle area in December 1941. The average age of ATS girls in the batteries was twenty-one, and there were about 200 in each battery.

The trials and early employment of the members of the ATS had been so satisfactory that the RA wanted, and certainly needed, to increase the number posted into mixed batteries. General Pile was told that the number of ATS was expected to rise and peak at around 220,000 at the beginning of 1943 and he could anticipate having 170,000 for his MBs. He later admitted that this figure had proved over-optimistic due to other army demands for ATS girls to contribute to the war effort. Anti-Aircraft Command only got around 74,000 at any one time.

In 1941 the BBC broadcast an appeal for kine-theodolite (KT) operators to serve with the ATS doing essential and secret work with the RA. Volunteers for this needed maths skills, good eyesight and physical fitness to cope with working in the open air. At officer level they were expected to have a BSc degree. 'Kine-girls' of the ATS worked with the RA to improve the precision of anti-aircraft fire.

Hilda's Story

Hilda Mitchell's (née Grant) story was typical of many girls of the time, both before and after she joined the ATS.

Hilda had been born and bred in Cleethorpes, Lincolnshire. When scarcely into her teenage years she was taken out of school by her father because her mother had died and there were other siblings to look after, a house to run and meals to put on the table. Even as she grew up her father wouldn't let her leave home. Eventually, at twenty-two years of age and after two brothers had joined the navy and a sister had married, Hilda herself left and enlisted in Grimsby.

Hilda Mitchell (née Grant) with Herbert on their wedding day.

Her subsequent posting to Wales to train as a Royal Artillery Ack-Ack (Anti-Aircraft) recruit was the farthest she had ever travelled in her life.

Hilda's background before her enlistment is a reminder of why the Home Postal Centre of the Royal Engineers (RE) played such an important role in service life. Her future husband Herbert was serving in India with a friend whose locker door was full of pictures of girls from his old school in Cleethorpes, all of whom seemed to keep the Forces Post Office quite busy. However, sadly, Herbert didn't have anybody writing to him. The friend took pity on him and said he could choose a photo and write to that girl; so he did and the girl was Hilda. They corresponded for five years before actually meeting just after Hilda had joined the ATS. They married six weeks later; it was a real 'wartime wedding' with both of them in uniform – the khaki being relieved only by Hilda's bouquet. She became pregnant immediately so left her training with the RA.

Although she served for only six months, she left with the same memory as other ATS girls – that of a very different experience with a friendly group of colleagues. They had sat in their barrack room in the evenings embroidering a tablecloth, which came in handy as a wedding present for Hilda. She kept that memento all her life.

There was one aspect of their duties that the ATS 'gunner girls' didn't talk about much. Some of them, like Hilda, had to come to terms with the idea that their objective was to enable the shooting down and killing of aircrew who were probably much like our own RAF fighters – young, with families who were at home worrying about them. Anyone who was liable to think along these lines, albeit briefly like Hilda, then remembered that they were helping to defeat an enemy who wanted to destroy Britain and her way of life. That soon put everything back into perspective.

Guns and Physical Training

Elizabeth Hansen (née Trattles) was a sales lady in the handbag department of the new Emporium of the Middlesbrough Co-operative Society. She then started her ATS career in a rather unusual way. Elizabeth enlisted on 26 December 1941, at the Wesleyan Chapel, where she had already worn 'uniform' as a Brownie and a Girl Guide, and where she went to Sunday School. She was just twenty years old.

As a recruit she was sent to the training camp at Glencorse Barracks in Pennicuik, just south of Edinburgh, arriving on 2 January 1942. Like so many ATS girls who served through winters in basic accommodation, Elizabeth found it very cold – but realised it wasn't such a shock to her because she was a northerner and used to freezing weather.

Her results in the selection tests, which everyone went through as a recruit to determine what trade or duties would be appropriate for them, enabled her to follow the path of those chosen to train with the RA as 'gunner girls'.

First of all she went to Park Hall Camp in Oswestry to start her training; then off to a gun site on the Yorkshire coast at Saltwick Bay, Whitby, billeted in the Angel Hotel. To get to work each day the girls climbed the famous 199 steps in full battledress to get to the East Cliff. That's a tough commute!

Elizabeth seemed to be following the routine path of ATS gunner girls when she later moved to 515 (M) HAA Battery. As a corporal she served in the Bristol area in an RA Searchlight unit, organising the ATS girls on their twenty-four-hour shift system.

However, she actually took on a second job to become a sergeant physical training instructor (Sgt PTI). So she had two jobs – height and range finder with the RA and PTI, although she was well aware which of those was the most important. Details of the Army Physical Training Corps appear later. Elizabeth has her own memories of it: 'Our PT kit was awful, brown shorts and orange top; The girls didn't care much for that or for PT, Sometimes my call of "everybody out" caused a few groans.'

Elizabeth married during the war and, at its end, went to Fulford Barracks in York to be demobbed.

Guns and More Physical Training

Elizabeth might well have been directed into her PT training by Eleanor Gibson. Eleanor had been selected to serve with the RA after basic training at Highlegh Hall in Knutsford, Cheshire. With a choice of trades she elected to become a clerk and was posted to the RA AA Group at Kimberley in Nottingham to work with three PT instructors – an ATS junior commander and two male instructors. The RA Group at Stanmore would send details of which battery personnel were to carry out PT training. Eleanor was then responsible for notifying those involved and sending the instructors out to various locations.

Guns, Biscuits and Tea

Joan de-Vall (née Crane) felt quite at home in military surroundings – literally – because she lived at Glen Parva Barracks in Leicester, where her father served with the Leicestershire Regiment.

Whereas some ATS recruits went to Glen Parva for basic training, Joan, already living there, was sent to Pontefract in Yorkshire – a typical army manoeuvre. Later, however, one benefit of living on top of the shop, as it were, was that whenever she returned home on leave she could, if necessary, go into the army pay office at Glen Parva for her wages.

As so often happened Joan's first experience of being in the ATS was meeting a group of other recruits at the railway station. That pleased everyone – 'safety in numbers' on a strange journey to a new way of life.

Amongst all the usual shocks of army life in basic training Joan remembers the beds. Ask an ex-ATS girl about biscuits and she won't offer you a plate of chocolate digestives but, like Joan and her old colleagues, will start to giggle over the ATS 'biscuits'. They were three small square mattresses that, together, stretched more or less over the length of the base. The trick for keeping them together during the night was to wrap them tightly in a blanket – but if there was only one blanket issued it was needed as a cover, not a base, along with an issue greatcoat in winter.

Joan admits that slowly but surely she succeeded in shaping up and falling into the routine of ATS army life. After the usual selection tests for aptitude, maths and literary skills Joan's posting instructions arrived – the RA training centre at Park Hall, Oswestry.

There she was trained in aircraft recognition and all the skills needed by ATS 'gunner girls' including what she calls 'shouting' or, more correctly, vocal training, i.e. how to call the firing orders to the men on the guns.

Then on to a practice firing camp in Wales. These camps allowed trainees to use their newly acquired academic skills for real, directing gun fire at textile 'sleeves' that billowed out behind small planes. When fully qualified, Joan was posted down to Falmouth above St Mawes in Cornwall, on to Plymouth and then down to Greenford. This large RAOC depot was in the London area and therefore suffered from German V-1 bomb attacks in 1944. One of these hit an ATS squad that was marching from their camp to the depot. Over fifty girls were injured, with some of them being admitted to hospital.

Interestingly, there was Joan serving in RA (M) HAA batteries around the coastline and in London, defending Britain against damage and possible invasion but, as we now say, that was just a day job; hard, tiring and dangerous but no more than thousands of her ATS colleagues did every day. After all, her father was the eldest of seven sons who all served in the army. What the ATS veteran Joan remembers most vividly are the times spent off duty and what life and people were like in those days.

People like the kind gentleman and young boy who gave up their seats on a Leicester to Grantham bus to Joan and one of her young uncles when they were both on leave. 'You young people have so little time together,' the gentleman said and they couldn't bring themselves to embarrass him by explaining their true, family relationship. Although this caused a laugh at the time Joan has never forgotten the kindness of that gentleman and boy.

They hitched lifts home at the end of the day – two offers of help to cover the whole journey but both equally appreciated. The first lift was in the smart car of an RAF officer and his wife; the second in a coal lorry. 'Life', as Joan says, 'was a wonderful experience'.

Except for the sad days when a dreaded telegram would arrive for somebody in the same accommodation hut. Missing or killed in action or died in an air crash. The fiancés, husbands, brothers, fathers – gone forever. Joan recalls that all they could do for their companion was to get her necessary kit together so that if they were called out on emergency duty the bereaved girl could carry on but on autopilot, as Joan describes it, 'with the light gone from her eyes'.

Within an ATS platoon or company there would have been girls who probably would not have been friends in civilian life or shared the same interests. Life in the ATS brought them together. Joan remembers that, on the last trip to the cookhouse at night, somebody always made sure that mugs of cocoa were brought back to the hut and stood on the top of the round stove for anyone who was late back off duty.

Her final memory is of long train journeys, packed like sardines, more often than not standing all the way. 'I don't know how they did it but whenever and wherever we arrived who would be waiting with wonderful mugs of hot tea to help us on our way? The Sally Ann – God bless them for not forgetting us.'

Searchlights and Anti-Freeze

Joan Riddell (née Blakey) went from basic training in Pontefract, Yorkshire, to Kinmel camp near Rhyl, North Wales, to train as a searchlight operator with the RA. A dozen or so ATS girls went from there to Buckinghamshire, where, as Joan puts it:

> We were welded into an efficient unit manning our first Searchlight Battery. It was not without incident I may say as on one occasion during the winter of 1943 we couldn't get the generator to start and someone suggested draining the cooling system. Of course it was full of the correct solution of anti-freeze and caused a bit of a problem until we were able to get the maintenance unit from the nearest Ack-Ack Battery to come and sort things out.

This original team of a dozen ATS went as a group to operate a searchlight in Tooting Beck, London – dangerous times, as Joan calls them, because the doodlebug bombing had just started.

Joan was involved in yet another area of historical innovation for the ATS. There had been concerns about ATS auxiliaries operating searchlight batteries but just about the time that Joan joined the ATS in 1942 previous experiments had proved successful and most of the worries had been dealt with, resulting in the formation of the 93rd Searchlight Regiment RA, manned by well over a thousand ATS searchlight operators like Joan.

A rare and rather blurred photograph of Joan Riddell (née Blakey) and Muriel Dobson with their searchlight. Courtesy of J. Riddell

Guns and Dancing

Olive Kinghorn (née Helyer) had waited for her official call-up papers before she joined the ATS in 1942, for a sad but not uncommon reason.

In 1941 her brother had died in a POW camp in Europe so, naturally, her family was still coming to terms with their loss.

Then, when the call came, Olive was off to Glencorse Barracks in Pennicuik, near Edinburgh. She remembers all the usual harsh realities of basic training – including the freezing cold winter weather.

She wanted to be either a driver or a PT instructor but neither option was available. The nearest she might get to it, according to advice, was as a part-time PTI on a gun site, so she went for that.

After training and a couple of early postings Olive arrived at 480 MB at Crownhill Barracks in Plymouth. A very active area but, as usual, everyone just got on with the job. Olive remembers training on a predictor and working as a plotter, determining the bearing of an aircraft in relation to the gun positions. She recalls that 'Plymouth was badly bombed and we saw action day and night. Our Major always commented on our dinky curlers under our steel helmets.'

The main attraction on off-duty days was the YWCA (Young Women's Christian Association) on the road up to the Plymouth Hoe. There might be music playing and at weekends they danced with sailors from Devonport. To keep a balance between rival services, local RAF boys would arrive for dances held in the NAAFI (Navy, Army and Air Force Institute). The girls had a wind-up gramophone and brought their own records from home.

Olive remembers the 1944 build-up to D-Day and the increased activity on the waters around Plymouth. There were DUKWs – an unpronounceable coded acronym created by General Motors who had manufactured what were always called 'ducks' – amphibious vehicles designed to carry goods or troops through water, overland or across landing beaches; and there were Sunderland flying boats.

After two and a half years in Plymouth Olive, a corporal by now, went to London and Buckhurst Hill in Essex when the bomb threat increased – the battery girls were now doing night guard, as the men did, and life was very busy but as Olive (and hundreds like her) said, 'We made the best of a scary situation'.

When the war ended and the MBs were disbanded work had to be found for Olive and all the ATS members in a similar position. What a contrast!

They were sent to a boys' school to serve lunches and to a day nursery to help out. Then to Yorkshire to be demobbed.

Olive repeats the conclusion of so many girls in khaki: 'One thing I do treasure was the comradeship and the friendships that endure to this day.'

Guns and Bagpipes

Betty Fleming had already started to do her bit by volunteering for fire-watching at her local youth club before she was old enough to join the ATS.

In 1942 her fiancé was posted to Burma so Betty immediately wanted to contribute towards 'getting the war over', as she explains it.

Coincidentally she heard that an old school friend had started to train for a special job in the ATS – on anti-aircraft guns; very secret work requiring slightly higher academic grades than usual. So Betty signed up and went off to basic training at Cameron Barracks in Inverness. There it seemed quite appropriate that the wake-up call was played on bagpipes by a piper whose favourite melody was 'Hey Johnnie Cope are ye wauking yet?'

Apart from that, basic training followed the set routines – including the usual parade-square misunderstanding which, this time, left one poor girl alone on the opposite corner of the square to everyone else.

From Betty's description Cameron Barracks seemed to boast a five-star cookhouse. Three good meals during the day and a buffet supper at about eight o'clock, which always included her favourite – trifle. She must have been one of the few recruits who managed to thwart the drill instructors by actually putting on weight despite all the square-bashing.

Betty did well in her selection tests and achieved her original objective of going to Oswestry to do Ack-Ack training. She eventually became a No. 1 on gun laying and remembers achieving the rank of lance sergeant before her RA duties finished at the end of the war and she was moved to the Pay Corps before being demobbed.

Guns and Beetroot

Despite all the difficult times we had I have always said, and still say, if I had my life to live over again I would still go back into the Army. It was a very good life.

So said Jane Savage (née Ritchie) when recounting her wartime experiences.

She was another Cameron Barracks recruit, travelling to Inverness from Aberdeen with a girl whom she'd met at the station, waiting for the same train, at 6.30 a.m. This recruit was W/125201 Jessie Ann Johnstone, who became an ATS Ack-Ack predictor operator with 538 and 350 (M) HAA batteries. They remained friends until 2004, when Jessie died.

So Jane, like Betty, had tales of the early-morning piper and the race for the bathroom and the breakfast parade ahead of the long queues. When it came to being issued with their uniforms the outfitters were males and didn't resort to any sophisticated questions like 'What size are you?' According to Jane, 'they just looked and then handed all the regulation kit over the counter, except for shoes which were deemed worthy of a size-question'.

The ATS girls were persuaded to do everything they were told and to obey all orders by the simple expedient of telling them to look the other way if they saw any soldiers running at the double with orders being shouted at them continuously because they were being punished for doing something wrong!

Their journey to the RA training camp at Devizes was the usual story of changes and delays and thirty-six hours to reach their destination.

For Jane it was the beetroot sandwiches that made this a different experience. An ATS sergeant gave them the sandwiches at the start, telling the girls not to eat them all at once because they had to last for a long journey. In fact Jane didn't eat them at all because she hated beetroot. So, by the time they were offered a hot meal on their arrival at Devizes, thirty-six hours later, she didn't feel well and couldn't eat the hot meal either. In the end she just fainted from lack of food, but doesn't record any of the remarks made by permanent staff who must have wondered how such a delicate flower would survive out on a cold and windswept gun site.

Of course, she did survive – even when posted to the firing-practice camp up on the East Cliff at Whitby, which required the morning climb up the town's famous 199 steps. Soon Jane was a predictor operator with 535 (M) HAA Battery, where she met her future husband.

From Whitby she went south, ending up in Dulwich in outer London. Her (M) HAA Battery was alongside a rocket site and an ammunition dump holding their first-line ammunition.

Here was an example of how suddenly so-called off-duty activities could be overtaken by events in a dangerous location. As Jane recalls:

One night we had a dance in the NAAFI during which the alarm went off. Well, as usual, we all ran down to the Command Post. The bombs were dropping. We knew they were close but didn't know just how close. The rocket site got it and a few soldiers were killed. It was very upsetting for us especially as one soldier was going on leave next day to get married, and he was one of those who were killed.

Jane and her fiancé were married in July 1942, very soon after they met, and he was then posted to Palestine. Jane left the service from her posting at Dulwich because she was pregnant.

Defending Antwerp

In late 1944 and early 1945 members of some ATS/AA mixed batteries were posted overseas to Belgium to take part in the defence of Antwerp.

Having succeeded in the invasion of France on D-Day, with the subsequent move northwards through Normandy and on up to Paris, by the latter half of 1944 the main object of 21st Army Group was to cross the Rhine and take the industrial area of the Ruhr in Germany.

There was an obstacle to this plan – namely the huge port of Antwerp and its access from the coast via the Scheldt Estuary. The vital importance of this area was known to both sides in the war and they were going to fight for it with as many resources as they could muster after years of conflict. It was the main port of entry for British supplies and reinforcements which were running low. The American 1st Army was also suffering from lack of supplies.

By this time the Allies were virtually out of France and up on the borders of Belgium and Holland. However, without a major port in the north and with only small ports on the coast of France, the British Army was having to bring its supplies overland in lorries from Normandy – not only slow but a heavy drain on petrol supplies. Consequently Germany increased its bombing raids on Antwerp, and the surrounding area, using V-1s.

Field Marshall Montgomery halted the push for the Rhine until the provision of supplies via the Scheldt Estuary and the docks at Antwerp could be secured. The Allies best, if not only, plan of action was to increase the anti-aircraft artillery in defence of Antwerp. Hence the move overseas of ATS Ack-Ack girls.

Eileen Sharp (née Horobin) was one of these girls. She had done a great deal of travelling before she joined the ATS as she had been born in Simla, in

Eileen Horobin. Note the white lanyard and RA badge. Courtesy of P. Sharp.

India, where her father was serving with the Royal Horse Artillery. After they returned to England they eventually settled in Syston in Leicestershire. Sadly, Eileen died in 2001 but her memories are kept alive by her family.

Eileen worked in Leicester for the Clarks shoe company but was keen to join the ATS – a venture about which her parents weren't very happy. Undeterred, she went out during one lunch hour and signed on.

Her parents were concerned about the loss of her wages as she had several siblings and money was always in short supply. Fortunately for the family, Eileen used the ATS pay-day facility whereby she could arrange for a certain amount from her pay to be sent home every week.

She served in anti-aircraft mixed batteries as a height-finder and, after D-Day, was in the first mixed battery to go to the defence of Antwerp during the heavy bombing by Germany. To be allowed to join that first battery Eileen reputedly let her two corporal's stripes go. She and her ATS colleagues had a narrow escape when travelling to their weekly bath parade in Antwerp; their lorry had just cleared the entrance to a tunnel when a bomb hit it.

She shared similar experiences in Belgium that have been recalled by other ATS members: the kindness of civilians; the off-duty hours spent in the Montgomery Club in Brussels; the black market in food that was badly needed by local people who just couldn't afford the high prices.

After the war ended in May 1945 Eileen served on for another six months in Germany where she saw in sharp outline the devastation that war brings amongst the ruins of Hamburg, where so many of the dead were those who were either too young or too old to fight in the military services, as well as gas chambers that were being demolished. She also travelled to the area around the Mohne Dam where there was a forces leave centre; there she saw

Eileen Horobin, South Shields, November 1944. Practising for embarkation to Antwerp. Courtesy of P. Sharp.

Eileen Horobin with her friend Peggy in Brussels.
Courtesy of P. Sharp.

Eileen Horobin, *second on right*. Courtesy of P. Sharp.

Insignia patch of Anti-Aircraft Command.
Courtesy of P. Sharp.

Montgomery's card. Courtesy of P. Sharp.

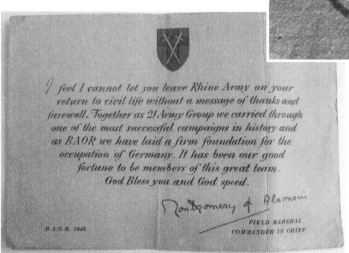

I feel I cannot let you leave Rhine Army on your return to civil life without a message of thanks and farewell. Together as 21 Army Group we carried through one of the most successful campaigns in history and as BAOR we have laid a firm foundation for the occupation of Germany. It has been our good fortune to be members of this great team. God Bless you and God speed.

Montgomery of Alamein

B.A.O.R. 1946

FIELD MARSHAL
COMMANDER IN CHIEF

the work that had been carried out to repair the dam and the damage caused to the surrounding countryside when the dam had been breached by skilled and brave British pilots.

Illustrated are her insignia patch of Anti-Aircraft Command and the card that Field Marshall Montgomery sent to all troops who had served with 21st Army Group. The photograph of the seven ATS girls (probably recruits in training) reveals other snippets. The girls came from Devon, London, Scotland, Cumberland, Manchester and Somerset. Quite a mixed bunch; but, despite some of the unkind comments about girls who wore khaki, Eileen wrote on the reverse of the card which she sent home, 'These are the girls in my hut, the most decent crowd of girls you could wish to meet'.

Eileen served for five years in the ATS; as a civilian she indulged in one small remembrance of those years. When she married John, an ex-Grenadier guardsman, in their home town of Syston their wedding cake sported a Grenadier Guards badge alongside an ATS one.

Girls in Eileen Horobin's hut – new recruits. Courtesy of P. Sharp.

Probably 554 Battery, mix of RA, ATS and troops of Royal Pioneer Corps, 1944 or 1945. The trophies at the front are: left – ATS 554 Battery 1944; middle – RA badge; right – Royal Pioneer Corps badge. Courtesy of P. Sharp.

The Royal Horse Artillery

Sybil Ward (née Topham) was one of those girls who joined the ATS 'by chance' in 1939, when she was eighteen years old. She lived in Leicester, where she met two Cockney sisters from London who had arrived in the town as recruits. They all remained friends during their service years and the sisters are part of the 'Guard of Honour' in Sybil's wedding photograph.

After training Sybil served with the Royal Horse Artillery (RHA) which had mountain batteries for duty in any hilly terrain which couldn't take wheeled traffic. Sybil's fondest memory was of doing drill training after her battery's horses had been replaced by as yet untrained mules. They escaped and caused chaos whilst troops on the parade ground remained standing to attention. Unfortunately there are no photographs of that event!

Sybil moved around with the RHA – to the Neville's Cross training centre in Durham and to Glasgow, where she was billeted with two other ATS girls in rooms over a garage. She also spent time at Edinburgh Castle with the Black Watch but never talked about her duties. She left the service in 1945 when the war ended.

Sybil was another girl in khaki who said, 'If I had the chance I'd do it all again'.

Sybil Topham, 1939. Courtesy of
B. Ward.

Sybil (née Topham) and Arthur Ward,
3 October 1942, on their wedding
day at St Leonard's Church, Leicester.
Courtesy of B. Ward.

With the Guns in Scotland

Lucy Bowyer (née Evans) went to Lancaster for her basic training, to Bowerham Barracks, then the home of the King's Own Regiment. Selected for training as an ATS Ack-Ack girl she went through the familiar routines at Park Hall Camp, Oswestry; what made her training a bit different was that she met her future husband there. When they married in the following year Lucy again followed what was becoming a familiar ATS tradition – she borrowed her wedding dress from a colleague.

Her early operational postings illustrated how the ATS (M) HAA batteries were guarding vital areas of the country well away from the South Coast defences against bombing and possible invasion.

Lucy served in Paisley, where the (M) HAA batteries were protecting shipping on the Clyde. The west coast ports of Glasgow and Liverpool were vital in providing facilities for the relatively safer shipping of stores, ammunition, mail and troops, especially to areas like the Middle and Far East.

She then went to 487/137 (M) HAA Regiment, protecting a large oil refinery at Ellesmere Port, just south of Liverpool. Lucy was a sergeant by the time the regiment moved to London, stationed partly in Hyde Park, where Winston Churchill's daughter Mary was an ATS battery officer.

January 1945 found Lucy and her comrades at Tilbury Docks, boarding SS Longford

Lucy Bowyer (née Evans). On camp guard duty with a spade at gun site, Paisley 1941. Courtesy of L. Bowyer.

Using equipment for targeting distance of guns, shows need for 'shouting' or vocal training. Courtesy of L. Bowyer.

The Polish Prime
Minister visits Lucy's
London battery
in 1943. Lucy
is standing in the
background, wearing
a white lanyard.
Courtesy of L. Bowyer.

HAA Battery ATS girls arriving at Luneburg Heath, May/June 1945. Courtesy of L. Bowyer.

June 1945, a Dakota taking Lucy Bowyer and fellow ATS girls from Antwerp to Luneburg, Germany.
Courtesy of L. Bowyer.

en route for Ostend, their final destination being Neerijse, where they took part in the defence of Antwerp.

When victory was won in Western Europe she, like so many others, was busy back-loading front-line equipment; she flew, by Dakota, to Luneburg Heath in Germany to continue this work. Her memories of Belgium and Germany are similar to those of other ATS girls who served there. In Belgium it was the kindness and generosity of a few families who had so little themselves but would provide warm drinks and food to cold, tired and hungry ATS members.

In Germany it was the ruins of Hamburg that left an impression, as well as the way in which women and children begged on the street or rummaged in bins for scraps of left-over food from Allied kitchens and cafes.

Lucy Bowyer outside her sleeping quarters in Germany, 1945. It is an unusual outfit for tent quarters, but she is just about to take part in a concert the ATS girls had arranged. Courtesy of L. Bowyer.

The ATS in North Wales

In 1939 the Coast Artillery School RA was based at Shoeburyness, on the Essex coast. By 1940 it faced three problems:

- ♦ Lack of capacity, given the increase in training and testing requirements imposed by the outbreak of war
- ♦ Potential exposure to air raids
- ♦ Its position in the path of a possible German invasion

The authorities, therefore, searched around the British coast to find a suitable, safer location – and they decided on Llandudno, the coastal resort in North Wales, particularly because of the position of the Great Orme, the high headland surrounded by sea. The Little Orme, at the opposite end of the sweeping bay, was also used.

The Mostyn family owned all the land; the Mostyn Trustees don't have in their archives any War Office documentation relating to the requisitioning of the site but doubt that there was any charge as the Ormes had no agricultural value. The land was returned to the Mostyn family in 1946.

During the war the 'Artillery Practice Ranges' in Llandudno were protected by a detailed set of by-laws about their use and, amongst other things, what local trophy-hunters were to do with any pieces of used armaments that they found. Today the remains of the RA buildings are protected by CADW, the official Welsh body responsible for the preservation of historic sites and buildings.

The new HQ of Coast Command was in the Gogarth Abbey Hotel, on West Shore, and close to the firing positions on the Orme itself. The hotel was also the senior officers' mess. There were over fifty girls in the ATS company in Llandudno, working in the Gogarth Abbey Hotel. Houses were requisitioned in the town for the ATS, who experienced kindness from local civilians.

ATS recruits who had done their initial training in RA training centres went on to Ty Croes on Anglesey for the next stage – firing practice, using the instruments to target the 'sleeves' billowing behind small aircraft.

Norman Longmate, in his book *The Doodlebugs*, pays tribute to the ability of the ATS Ack-Ack girls to cope with whatever their duties brought them. In his account of the intensive V-1 bombing of the South Coast areas he tells us: 'The supposedly "weaker sex" were as hard pressed as the men.' 'Life was one long rush up and down from the gun park,' remembers a former ATS radar operator with a heavy AA battery at Minster, near Sheerness. 'We had to sleep with our plimsolls on and no sooner did we strip off to have a wash than the alarm bells would sound again.'

He continues:

Women proved better able than men to fill the tedious periods of waiting in between the frenzied moments of action. On a gun-site close to the river Medway there was a sudden craze for embroidery and one former member of the ATS remembers sitting quietly stitching away, while awaiting the call to action. 'I lost no end of needles jumping up each time the alarm went. Now, thirty-two years later (this account is from 1976), I still have not finished one of those tablecloths.'

Final Salute

In 1955 a model silver gun was presented by General Sir Frederick Pile in commemoration of the huge contribution made by those members of the ATS who served with his Anti-Aircraft Command. Brigadier Mary Railton, then Director WRAC, accepted the model on behalf of the corps.

Four

Alongside the Corps of Royal Engineers

The Army Postal and Courier Service

Compared with the overwhelming need for secrecy in certain branches of the army, it's not immediately obvious why mail services should be considered as secret operations, until the background and organisation are examined more closely.

Some ATS felt that letter-sorting wasn't one of the most 'glamorous' of wartime occupations until they remembered their biggest morale-booster – a quotation reputed to come from General Montgomery who said that his men could march for three days without food if sustained by one letter from home.

During peace and wartime the Corps of Royal Engineers (REs) were responsible for running the Army Post Office (APO). The tradition of being ably assisted by girls in khaki went back to the First World War, when women in the WAAC/QMAAC served with the APO.

At the start of the Second World War the Army Postal Service operated out of the long-established civilian sorting office at Mount Pleasant in London. The first consignment of mail for British troops in France left there on 14 September 1939. The space available in the depot was obviously going to be inadequate and there was the possibility of disruption from bombing of buildings and transport routes, so the Army Postal Service moved to Reading. Its stay there was less than two months as it again outgrew the space available. Significantly, however, that was where the girls in khaki first turned up to help out. This time it was the 10th Berkshire Coy of about sixty members with a junior commander in charge. The company provided cooks, clerks, orderlies and typists – the traditional trades that the ATS had initially been expected to provide.

When Reading quickly proved to be unsuitable the Army Postal Service had to decide where to go next – on what was expected to be its final move. There was Bournemouth or there was Nottingham. They chose Bournemouth – considered a safe area and convenient because of its proximity to the southern ports. That was before defeat in France, the evacuation of British troops from Dunkirk to the South Coast, the hiatus in mail dispatches to France and the increase in those to the Middle East. One way or another everything that happened in the war had an effect on army (and RAF) postal services and their organisation.

So the final move was made to Nottingham, now considered suitable because of its inland location in the Midlands, its good rail connections for the mail trains that arrived and left day and night, and its greater proximity to the west-coast northern ports of Liverpool and Glasgow, which were

ATS members of the Home Postal Centre, Nottingham, outside Trent Bridge cricket club, where those who were billeted in requisitioned houses had their mess, 21 June 1944. Kneeling at the very end on the right (facing) is Muriel Standidge (Stanny), finally promoted to CSM. On left, bottom row, fifth in is Corporal Margaret Croft, later promoted to sergeant. The small lad behind them is unknown! Courtesy of B. Danter.

being used for mail dispatches to the Middle East. Nottingham also offered around 140 factories and other buildings that were requisitioned as mail-sorting depots, administrative offices, catering facilities, messes and billets. By now ATS girls were training as postal staff.

The best-known requisitioned buildings included the famous Trent Bridge cricket ground and the Palais de Dance for messing arrangements, and the Vyella Factory as a sorting office. Billets were found in Arkwright Street, West Bridgford, Bulwell Drill Hall and the wooden huts at the rear of Wilford House. The operation in Nottingham was designated the Home Postal Centre (HPC).

One ATS girl was born and bred within easy reach of many of the new sites, so considered herself lucky to be selected for the HPC.

Barbara Danter (née Miller) enlisted in Nottingham, went to Glen Parva Barracks in Leicester for basic training and then, after the usual recruit selection tests, she was sent back to Nottingham to join the HPC.

Training lasted for six weeks resulting in payment of 2s 6d per day and the right to wear the RE bomb on the left breast of the tunic. Officers of the APO were always informed in advance about proposed troop move-

ments; mail could then be held for forwarding to the appropriate field post office in the new location so that soldiers received their 'letters from home' as soon as they arrived – hence the need for the Official Secrets Act. This even applied to the D-Day operational plans. It's amazing to think that while the whole of southern England was crammed with British troops waiting, with their Allied counterparts, for the signal to start the invasion, their mail was already

Barbara Danter as a recruit, 1945.
Courtesy of B. Danter.

'A' Section ATS Home Postal Centre, 1944, outside Trent Bridge cricket ground, Nottingham. Front row: centre (with glasses) Major McCloud, his left (facing) CSM Cooley, his second left Sgt M. Denne ATS and on his right CSM Dixon ATS. Courtesy of B. Danter.

packed and on the ships waiting to follow them over the Channel, so that when they reached their first base their letters from home would be there as well. Not an easy task as postal supervisors had to work on the beaches, checking what each ship was carrying and for which units.

All this was achieved through the use of a coded address system. All correspondence showed only: rank and name, unit, APO England. Senders, even Next of Kin (NOK), didn't know where their letters were going to. When the GPO collected these items they simply passed them on to Nottingham – by the lorry load!

HPC operators like Barbara had to learn all the 'shorthand' for army locations and units and the position of all the appropriate pigeon holes in the sorting office. The aim was to process 1,000 letters an hour – for that there was a small increase in pay.

The girls grew skilled at securing carelessly wrapped parcels and deciphering badly addressed mail. This obviously happened in civvy street as well. British Railways had difficulties with badly addressed parcels. The problem was usually that, because of wartime shortages, senders were re-using old wrapping paper without obscuring previous addresses. Traders were also asked to show clearly the destination station from which deliveries would be collected. British Railways took out adverts to reinforce their instructions about clear labelling.

The most upsetting incidents in the HPC were the receipts of blood-stained returned mail from units that had been attacked, as happened when a base APO in Belgium was hit by a doodlebug. Such mail was always retained until the NOK, or the sender, had been told of the death officially.

Barbara remembers working on night shifts when the meal break came at about 0100 hours. She and her friends would eat in the basement of the Nottingham Palais, under the dance floor.

The HPC had a wide range of other responsibilities. It was the recruitment and training centre for postal staff; it provided reinforcements and stores for field post offices; it ran the APO records office and the accountancy centre.

It was particular about adding both RE and ATS badges to all announcements, entertainment programmes and party menus. It was especially meticulous about the welfare of its female staff. Party or Christmas dinner menus, for example, always carried the extra notice that the (tough?) RE staff would have beer while the (fragile?) ATS would have minerals.

The Dukeries of Nottinghamshire

Like many auxiliaries who were no longer needed in their wartime role at the end of hostilities, Barbara Danter left the Home Postal Centre in Nottingham. Again like many, she was sent to another location where ATS worked and where she might be occupied. Barbara went to Welbeck Abbey, the ancestral home in north Nottinghamshire of the dukes of Portland which was by then designated as a Formation College. The duke and duchess had carried on living in part of the abbey during the war, the remainder being taken over by the War Office for various purposes associated with officer training. A local resident remembers officers being posted there, still with their horses, which were accommodated in the late nineteenth-century riding house and stables. Cavalry regiments carried out horse training there – mechanisation of cavalry regiments wasn't completed until 1937 and not all the privately owned horses disappeared immediately. One outstanding feature of the abbey is the underground ballroom, built around 1870. During the war it housed the library and the duke's personal treasures.

Officers studied in the library but Barbara used to accompany those who wanted to see some of the exhibits. Then she operated the telephone switchboard for some months before being demobbed in 1947. What she didn't know was that there was an ATS link between Welbeck and nearby Clumber Park, which had been the ancestral home of the dukes of Newcastle, making it another of 'the Dukeries'. The park covered nearly 4,000 acres of agricultural land, grassland, heathland and forestry, so there was no way in which it was going to escape War Office requisitioning in 1939. The park area was ideal for ammunition storage in the standard 'Shelters IG' – Shelters Iron-Galvanised – which could be spaced out according to pre-determined safety limits. Like the famous Nissen and Romney huts, they were transported as flat packs but were open-ended when their twenty-one pieces were erected. Clumber Park was just one example of the hundreds of ammunition storage sites in use throughout Britain.

The physical link between Welbeck and Clumber involved tea – probably in urns this time. The wife of the Duke of Portland's elderly cook at Welbeck used to take a vehicle across to Clumber and distribute tea to the men working on the ammunition storage sites. The ATS link was that girls in khaki were stationed at Clumber and accommodated in the stable block. Some were carrying out clerical and secretarial duties for the HQ staff; others were drivers moving ammunition to and from the specially adapted small railway station near the local village of Ranby, which was used for the ammunition trains whose contents would be inspected on unloading to ensure that they hadn't been damaged in transit – a task not suitable for the local railway station in Worksop.

Clumber Park was bought by the National Trust in 1946, although some of the ammunition was still being back-loaded to the major CADs (Central Ammunition Depots) in the early fifties.

Five

Alongside the Royal Corps of Signals

*H*undreds *of* ATS girls served with the Royal Corps of Signals as telephonists, teleprinter operators, switchboard operators – all the functions that provided the British Army with its communications network.

Signals and Lions

Kay Gardner Bergl reminisces about her time in signals when stationed at the War Office in Whitehall between 1944 and 1946. Or, rather, her time off-duty during those years. As she says:

> I remember we were always able to go to any theatre in London and be given free tickets, many times in front seats. I was fortunate enough on one occasion to see Vivien Leigh and Laurence Olivier. Also while at the War Office, during the bombings, we had to leave our billets in Victoria and travel by bus to underground bunkers in a suburb for safety. One morning on the bus provided for us to return to work in Whitehall, a V-1 'Doodlebug' started to fly over us prior to the usual descent. The driver of the bus said to us 'Well girls, do I stop driving, or do we go on?' The response was unanimous 'go on', which we did. The bomb fell somewhere behind us!
>
> On VE day, May 8 1945, I came off duty at midday at the War Office and walked to Trafalgar Square, which was filling up rapidly with crowds of happy

people. I was fortunate enough to be lifted up by a U.S. soldier to sit on one of the lions and spent many happy hours with the crowds celebrating the occasion.

Kay was later posted to Germany and recalls the journey:

I remember the train I was on with many other ATS girls en route to General Montgomery's BAOR HQ. The trains operating in Germany at that time were only for the use of our forces. We were given big packets of sandwiches to be eaten en route. However, every time the train stopped for any reason dozens of little children would come begging at the train windows and, of course, most of us gave away our sandwiches.

Different Life – Same Job

Jean Sperry (née Ball) joined the ATS in 1945, having become unsettled in her civilian life. She was a switchboard operator so there was no problem over finding her an 'ATS trade'. That didn't mean, however, that she could escape several weeks of basic training at Guildford. Jean is happy to admit that she did avoid what might have been typical military humour, thanks to her father changing his name in the First World War by knocking off the 's' at the end of Ball! This was a further advantage when it came to drill sessions, because Jean just couldn't get the hang of changing step on the march. So the order that bellowed out across the parade ground when Jean, yet again, had made a bit of a mess of this tricky manoeuvre was 'Fall out Ball'. Though, only as far as the drill shed which had a mirror at each end so that Jean could watch herself in action.

Released from this not-uncommon purgatory, she was posted to Catterick, in Yorkshire, the home of the Royal Corps of Signals, to Devizes and then on as a telephonist to the signals station between Hillingdon and Uxbridge on the outskirts of London. This base liaised with No. 11 Fighter Group RAF, Uxbridge, which flew Hurricanes and Spitfires, passing on information about flight paths, etc.

Like all her ATS colleagues Jean took her duties very seriously but still managed to retain a sense of humour about well-remembered off-duty incidents. Like the time when, as a member of the unit's entertainment committee, she helped to organise a coach party to Brighton with an officer in charge. Jean sat next to the officer in a restaurant that provided a lovely roast dinner. She stuck her fork into a roast potato only for it to shoot straight off the plate and into the officer's lap.

On night duty as telephonists the girls naturally made tea. The crockery had to be washed up the next morning in washrooms/toilets that they shared with the men. Leaning over the basins on washing-up duty, the girls in khaki didn't dare look round when one or two men came in to relieve themselves. 'All in a day's work,' Jean recalls. 'Mind you, we had trousers on so maybe they thought we were one of the men.'

From the Highlands of Scotland to a Famous Normandy Beach

Elizabeth Grogan served in the ATS from 1942 to 1946. During that time she experienced typical aspects of life in the service, from endless slow journeys and rotten ablutions (the army term for washing and toilet facilities) to dances and the sights of war-torn European countries. She tells her story in her own words:

I was conscripted into the ATS in December 1942 and sent to Talavera Camp in Northampton for basic training. I was then posted to Strathpeffer (in the Scottish Highlands) for signals training – teleprinting and switchboard operating and signals office procedure. I was the only one going to Strathpeffer so a corporal was assigned as my escort and after several train stoppages etc it took 27 hours to reach our destination, having spent the night on the train. I was billeted at the Ben Wyvis Hotel and trained at the Highland Hotel.

I was then posted to Western Command HQ Chester and remained there until 1944. One day my name went up on orders to have a kit inspection. After the officer had finished I asked, 'Why have I had this inspection?' and she replied, 'don't you know, then let me be the first to congratulate you, you are going to COSSAC!' This meant nothing to me – COSSAC stood for Chiefs of Staff to the Supreme Allied Commander (designate). I duly arrived in London and met up with others who had come from different units. My friend, with whom I still correspond, came from Leamington Spa central Midlands District. The females were taken to a temporary billet – a big house in Catherine Place off the Buckingham Palace Road. We were there for a short while and then moved to a hostel owned by Bourne & Hollingworth – the big London store. This was near Goodge Street underground station and it was below the station itself that we began our editing training. It was very scary hearing the trains above your head. At this time the Doodlebugs were coming over London. As long as you heard them you were alright, but when their humming noise stopped you dived for cover.

On 14th February Eisenhower was appointed as Supreme Commander and the next day COSSAC became SHAEF (Supreme HQ Allied Expeditionary Forces). SHAEF moved in March to Bushy Park near Kingston on Thames.

Army life with the Americans was very different from that with the British Army, we had the best of everything. Better quarters, better food and there was even a ballroom on site – no. 8 ballroom – Glen Miller's band was the unit band. There was a cinema/theatre & restaurant. We were in huts; according to a newspaper cutting I have there were approximately 400 huts and 5 office blocks. When SHAEF took over, Bushy camp had doubled to take 8,000 American troops.

When proceedings for D-Day got underway some of us were moved to SHAEF Forward at Plymouth. We were billeted in one of the forts along the coast – Fort Purbrook. The men were put inside and the females in tents in the moat, things were very different. Washing and toilet facilities were non-existent. There were chemical toilets around the moat and a shanty affair for a wash place open to the elements. Bowls were placed along a wooden plank and there was a big boiler. If you took water out you had to put the same amount back in, often there was more cold than hot! There were 4 beds to each tent.

In the editing section we received 'in' and 'out' messages from the teleprinting room, decoded messages from American code and deciphered messages from British cipher – all of which we had to 'edit'. That meant we had to put them into readable English according to a special format, afterwards we typed them out on electric typewriters and then sent them to Staff Messages Control for distribution. Messages ranged from Confidential, Secret, Top Secret & Eyes Only. We had to sign that we would not divulge anything which we read.

Then, soon after D-Day, we embarked on the troopship 'Cheshire' at Southampton for France. We landed at Omaha Beach where no one seemed to expect us. I will never forget being carried over the mud by US soldiers; they took us to their camp where we spent one and a half nights. We were in tents – 6 to a tent – sleeping 'top to tail'. Then, in darkness, we boarded 3-ton trucks and were taken on a long journey to Versailles. We were accommodated in an old French barracks – Satory Barracks. Again toilet arrangements were very primitive. Not even chemical ones except for nighttime. There were holes in the ground in a sectioned-off building affair. The 'Pilgrims of the Night' came to sort these out. Thankfully there were proper flush ones in the office where we worked directly opposite the Palace gates.

But there were compensations, being in signals we did shift work and we were in Paris every other day. When we had a 48-hour leave we were allowed to spend that at the Hotel Metropolitan in the Rue Cambon. Like it was in London, we were able to get tickets to see shows.

After the war ended on 7th May 1945 SHAEF was disbanded and the unit split up. Some were posted to Bad Oeynhausen, some to 30 Corps British Army Frankfurt in Germany. On June 19th I was in the group going to 1 Corps Iserlohn in Germany.

We went by truck to Buc airport and from there flew to Hannover. We then set out on an 8-hour truck ride through Germany. We were amazed at the devastation caused by the bombing raids – much worse than in England. Some of the Germans were hostile, booby traps were set across roads and we had an accident. There were two trucks – the kitchen and domestic staff were in the first one. I don't know quite what happened, but the truck overturned and some of the girls were injured, they were afterwards returned to England. We were in the 2nd truck and were taken to a convent while things were sorted out; the nuns were very kind to us and gave us black, sugarless coffee.

We arrived in Iserlohn at 0330 and were given beds in the men's barracks because our billets were not ready for us, Next day we moved into flats. I was not there long for on the morning of the 29th June I was told by someone coming off night shift that it had come through on the teleprinters that six of us were going back to Paris! We left Iserlohn the next day. The six of us, and our belongings, were in a 3-ton truck escorted by two officers in a jeep. Once again we passed through the blitzed cities and towns, crossed the Rhine at Cologne and had lunch there. Passed through Holland and Belgium and arrived in Brussels at 1800, there we spent the night. We left Belgium behind and into France reaching Paris late afternoon.

Next day we were told we would be with CALA (Combined Administrative Liquidating Agency). We were billeted at a girls' school in Montreuil Paris; we were joined by six more girls who had been posted to Frankfurt when SHAEF was dissolved.

I can't remember how long I was with CALA before being posted back to Germany, where I remained until I was demobbed. I was there for eight months before being demobbed in England in May 1946. I had spent 11 months in France.

My friend was killed in Germany, she was in a jeep going to a dance. A cable had been placed across the road which caused the jeep to overturn. We used to get many invitations to dances from various units. The German women used to do our washing, which they did beautifully. We gave them half a tablet of soap, which was very scarce. They didn't want money, we gave them cigarettes and chocolate.

Underground in London Again

Agnes Thomson (née Waters), also known as Scotty, became familiar with the underground signals offices at Goodge Street. She had trained at the Signals Training School based at Edinburgh University, where there was space during the war. She learnt Morse Code, teleprinter operations, signals procedures and codes and, finally, OKR (Operator Keyboard and Line Morse). Then it was off to Whitehall and Goodge Street, both of which had underground signals units.

From there Agnes went to 30 ATS Company at Luneburg and later on to the 21st Army Group at Bad Oeynhausen. In telling her story she points out that all the moving around that they did was not unusual because every unit had to have its own support from clerical and secretarial staff, signals staff, drivers, orderlies, cooks and medics. This came under the heading of the unit 'establishment' – the pre-determined scale of personnel by rank and qualification, vehicles, weapons and other equipment.

As it wasn't easy to travel home for short leave periods, the British Army set up leave camps in the German countryside for troop serving with BAOR (British Army of the Rhine).

Agnes went to a leave camp close by the Mohne Reservoir, looking down towards the Mohne Dam of 'Dambusters' fame. All kinds of leisure activities were provided and Agnes developed an interest and skill in horse riding, horse care and grooming.

She left the ATS in 1947 having met and married her husband in the space of a few weeks.

Signals and Intelligence

Careless Talk Costs Lives

The slogan appeared against various background illustrations, warning families, housewives and service personnel to guard against mentioning anything that might be useful to the enemy – from posting orders given to relatives to confidential documents seen by service personnel.

Thousands of ATS girls were bound by the Official Secrets Act (OSA) in ensuring that they didn't indulge in careless talk. In modern terminology we might say that the need for secrecy entered the DNA of those whose wartime occupations required absolute confidentiality.

It wasn't until the mid-1970s, when classified documents began to be released under the thirty-year rule, that details became known about the restricted activities of British intelligence and the words 'Enigma' and 'Ultra' entered everyday language. Even then, many ex-service personnel found it very difficult, if not impossible, to reveal what they had actually been doing during the war. It wasn't only the details of their work that couldn't be revealed under the OSA – it could also be the location of their unit.

Organisations that required a high degree of discretion in their teams, in addition to special qualifications, trawled through all the women's services to find suitable recruits who were then sent for interview without being given any details of what they would be doing if selected.

They would actually be working for the Royal Corps of Signals and the Intelligence Service (SIGINT in military terminology).

Bletchley Park

Amongst the many who needed neither posters nor the OSA to remind them of their duty were the personnel of Bletchley Park, known as Station X, and its outstations. The work done at Bletchley by its code-breakers was credited with shortening the war, but it also brought with it an understanding of the irreparable damage that could be done to Britain's future if they talked carelessly. Or, as Winston Churchill famously put it, they were 'the geese that laid the golden eggs, and never cackled'.

Bletchley Park itself had been built in the 1880s by Sir Herbert Leon, a banker and Liberal MP in the time of Gladstone. In 1938 the government took it over as the headquarters of the Government Code and Cypher School (GC & CS). Bletchley became the home of the 'code-breakers' – the teams working on the Ultra intelligence system designed to decode German military communications which were encrypted using a mechanical encoding machine called Enigma.

The largest contingent of women at Bletchley came from the Women's Royal Naval Service, but several hundred members of the ATS were also employed there, attached to the Intelligence Corps.

Kerry Johnson and John Gallehawk carried out a lot of research into the available statistics of the Bletchley operation throughout the war and published their findings in Figuring it out at Bletchley Park 1939–1945.

The recorded figures for ATS working in Bletchley Park were as follows:

1942

March	37
December	164

1943

January	152
December	335

1944

January	335
October	401 (Here the records started to show the breakdown of ATS between officers and other ranks (ORs). This total consisted of 70 officers and 331 ORs.)
December	411 (This was the peak of ATS personnel at Bletchley. The total consisted of 77 officers and 334 ORs.)

1945

January	410	(77 officers and 333 ORs.)
August	316	(51 officers and 265 ORs.)

Various off-duty activities went on at Bletchley Park for all operators and supporting staff. There could be evening lectures, tennis and other 'leisure activities'. Then there was eating!

Often overlooked in records of military units, catering statistics for Bletchley Park, included in Kerry and John's book, show what size of 'logistical exercise' it must have been. Having to cater for shift patterns meant that the caterers provided five types of meal per day from breakfast to a late-evening supper with at least one, and probably two, of the meals consisting of three courses. Plus an extra one at 0200 hours for the night shift.

Initially meals were taken in the main house – the Mansion – but a large canteen was built outside the grounds, for security reasons, in early 1942. That must have been eagerly awaited as over 10,000 meals a week were provided. By September 1943 this number had risen to almost 30,000 per week; rising to a peak of just over 32,000 by the end of June 1944 – the dates probably giving a clue as to the reason for that.

Amongst the ATS girls being fed at Bletchley Park was Betty Webb (née Vine-Stevens). In early 1941 Betty was a student at the Radbrook Domestic Science College in Shrewsbury; in common with so many women across the country Betty, and some of her fellow-students, felt that they ought to be doing something more positive for the war effort. This made it hard for them to settle into college life.

Betty's answer was to leave her studies and join the ATS on 3 September 1941 at the Royal Welsh Fusilier depot in Wrexham.

As Betty says:

> Leaving my comfortable, quiet life in the wilds of Herefordshire for the 'rough and tumble' of Army life hit me hard, but I soon accepted the fairly primitive living conditions and quite enjoyed basic training. However I did NOT enjoy having to help look for head lice amongst other recruits.

She soon learnt how to detect the lice. Treatment was as basic as the rest of life for many recruits. Those who had them were bound up in a paraffin-soaked head scarf and slept at one end of the hut.

Immediately following basic training Betty was sent to London to a selection interview for the GC & CS at Bletchley Park. She was posted there in October 1941 until February 1946, when Bletchley Park was closed and the organisation became what we now know as GCHQ – the Government Communications Headquarters.

Initially local houses, with their residents still at home, were required to take a few ATS girls from Bletchley. In some instances this led to over-crowding and very uncomfortable, cramped living conditions. It was not suitable either when operators were working late or night shifts. Betty suffered from such conditions when she first went to Bletchley and soon asked to be moved to better accommodation; she was then billeted, happily, in Loughton in what is now Milton Keynes. With the increasing number of operators at Bletchley this system of billeting just wasn't adequate, so a mixed camp was built nearby at Shenley.

Betty was a staff sergeant who remained at Bletchley Park until May 1945. For the first two years she was in the Mansion – the main building in the Park – in the military section. Then she moved to Block F to the Japanese military sub-section, paraphrasing deciphered Japanese signals.

This led to an intriguing interlude for her between May and October 1945 when she was posted to the USA – to the Pentagon in Washington DC where she was the only member of the ATS – to do that kind of work. Work with the same kind of secrecy attached to it. As Betty explains:

> I shared accommodation with other service girls but I had no idea what they did. We got up in the mornings and went off to work – but I didn't know where they went and none of us talked about our duties. Our conversations probably centred more on the availability of such lovely silk stockings!

They also must have touched on the warm weather conditions and the unsuitability of some items of British uniform – a Canadian girl took pity on Betty and lent her the Canadian uniform that she is wearing in the photograph.

Bletchley Park was a mixture of civilians recruited because they had some special skill, Foreign Office personnel and military staff (male and female) from all three services. Most personnel records were destroyed at the end of the war. To try to remedy this loss of information Bletchley Park Trust has set up a 'Roll of Honour' to obtain details of as many people as possible who worked there, at the outstations and in the Y Service.

Betty Webb (née Vine-Stevens) in Canadian uniform. Courtesy of B. Webb.

Not everyone at Bletchley was a code-breaker. ATS personnel listed on the Roll of Honour were doing other skilled work One of the special functions was 'Traffic Analysis' (TA), the technique of identifying signals for information about where transmissions emanated from, radio frequencies, call-signs and who sent them rather than the content of the encoded messages. In 1943 the various TA sections were merged into the department known as SIXTA. Others analysed the effects of weather conditions on transmission frequencies – this was known as Testery.

The Roll of Honour shows, for example, that Staff Sergeant Jeanne Henriette Lindley (née Cammaerts), who was ATS attached to the Intelligence Corps, worked in both these sections.

Corporal Helen Little ATS was at the park between 1942 and 1945; without exact records her 'Hut location' suggests that she was part of the SIXTA group doing traffic analysis. Several other ATS girls worked in the military section of SIXTA, named on the Roll, for example, as M.A. Macfadyen and M.J. Faskin.

Not all ATS members who served at Bletchley were employed in these specialist sections. Jean Campbell (née Macallister) worked at Bletchley in a clerical role for ten months between 1942 and 1943, then went to North Africa. Patricia Whittick (née Padbury) worked at Shenley as a teleprinter operator.

Each code-breaking hut had a registration room that provided the link with the Y Stations. Coded messages delivered from the Y Stations came first to this desk in the appropriate hut where they were logged and cross-referenced to build up a pattern of signals from the German armed forces.

In 2009 GCHQ gathered all available details of those who had worked at Bletchley Park so that the government could offer a commemorative badge to surviving veterans. It's significant that the reverse of the badge is inscribed 'WE ALSO SERVED'. Due to the secrecy involved in the work, many of those who carried it out found, post-war, that they were regarded as not having contributed very much to the 'war effort'.

The Y Service

Hundreds of ATS worked at the 'Y Stations' – the Signals Intelligence locations which intercepted enemy transmissions and passed them, still encoded, to Bletchley Park for decryption. They formed a network of wireless intercept stations situated around Britain and overseas. The War Office Y Stations most commonly mentioned by ATS intercept operators are Beaumanor in Leicestershire, designated the HQ of the network, Forest Moor near Harrogate and Kedleston in Derbyshire.

Radio intercept had been a possibility almost since radio transmissions were introduced at the end of the nineteenth century. It had been used effectively in some situations during the First World War, although, of course, it was still being developed. The CG & CS had existed since 1919 and the Admiralty had assumed responsibility for its operation and enhancement across all the services that used its output.

After the end of that earlier war, however, there was greater usage of intercept facilities by the diplomatic service than by military organisations. Due to this, by a strange coincidence in 1922 Lord Curzon, who was then Foreign Secretary in Lloyd George's government, decided that the CG & CS should come under the administrative control of the Foreign Office. He could never have imagined that, twenty years later, the Y Service with hundreds of ATS girls would be installed in his ancestral family home – Kedleston Hall in Derbyshire. Curzon was born there in 1859 and in what was described as one of the finest country houses in England.

An ancestor of Lord Curzon had been granted a peerage and baronetcy as Lord Scarsdale in 1761. In 1939 Richard Curzon, 2nd Viscount Scarsdale, offered Kedleston to the War Office. Kedleston was used by various military units including those who were assembling as part of the British Expeditionary Force en route to France.

There were between 400 and 500 ATS operators at Kedleston in No. 3 ATS wing of the Royal Signals and Intelligence Corps, although it was reputed to be the smallest of the stations. One of the first arrivals in 1942 was Squad 26 out of the training centre at Trowbridge. Kedleston Hall now belongs to the National Trust who have published a small but very interesting booklet about the hall and estate during the war, entitled 'Secrets and Soldiers'. A section devoted to the ATS members of the Y Service at Kedleston answers a couple of questions that are often asked. Why 'Y' stations? Apparently this is simply 'a phonetic derivation of W I – Wireless Intercept'. It had its origins in the First World War.

Secondly, why Station 'X' for Bletchley Park? This was 'not a code name but actually Station 10 in Roman numerals. There were a number of clandestine MI6 wireless stations and inside the attic storey of Bletchley Park mansion was number ten.'

One benefit of life at Kedleston for the Y Service ATS was the beautiful surrounding countryside of Derbyshire, especially for those who had bicycles with them. The booklet 'Secrets and Soldiers' contains personal memories of some of the ATS girls who served there. Apart from the secret work they were doing, their memories reflect those of the ATS in general: the very 'basic' quality of the food; the manipulation of the famous '3 biscuits' that formed a mattress; the dances; the kindness of civilians; and the trips into the local town (in this case Derby) for entertainment when the rigorous shift system allowed; the winter temperature of the accommodation huts; the meagre supply of fuel for the single 'central heating' stove in each hut; and the ways found to supplement the basic ration. We're talking here about ATS girls amongst whom initiative was a very desirable characteristic!

It's claimed that the successful operations by the code-breakers of the British Ultra intelligence system and the Y Service interceptors who fed them the encrypted transmissions saved millions of lives and shortened the war.

As an example of their achievements, the military historian John Keegan points out in his early account of the Battle of Normandy that the German Commander Rommel was making decisions about the timing of the deployment of German troops just after D-Day on 6 June 1944, using his divisional radios. Unknown to them, as John Keegan reveals, 'As soon as they had come on air, however, their transmissions had been picked up by the British monitoring service and the intercepts subjected to Traffic Analysis'.

As at Bletchley Park not all the ATS girls employed in the Y Service were specialist interceptors. Joyce Robertson (née Bahr) was at Beaumanor and Bishops Waltham between 1943 and 1945 as a driver. Her duties included delivering dispatches to Bletchley Park. There were teleprinter operators and typists at Beaumanor.

Many intercept operators tracked specific frequencies. For example Joan Melman (née Bellamy) who worked at Forest Moor in 1944/45 intercepted Luftwaffe traffic in Italy. Joan Sheppard (née Cromar-Mahon), an intercept operator at Shenley, picked up communications from the Gestapo HQ in Berlin. Another ATS operator worked against the German SS in Budapest and yet another monitored the German retreat through Italy.

So much of Second World War history came in via wireless headphones clamped to the ears of ATS girls!

Moreen's Story

W/2731587 Moreen Moss (née Head) had first-hand experience of the Y Service. She joined the ATS from the Civil Service and was sent to Glen Parva Barracks in Leicester for her basic training. Moreen obviously did well in some relevant part of the selection tests that recruits went through, although she wasn't very sure of the reason why she was posted to the Isle of Man to train for the Y Service. Moreen recounts how:

Moreen Moss (née Head) on the beach in Douglas, Isle of Man. No escape from uniform during what she call her 'overseas service'. Courtesy of M. Moss.

We were billeted in commandeered hotels on the seafront – known as Palace Camp and the course lasted almost six months. We were given our training in squads of 30, men and women, and at the end of the course I was kept on as a Lance Corporal Instructor, eventually made up to Corporal. I was married in December 1944 to a Lancaster air gunner Warrant Officer, who later won the Distinguished Flying Cross (DFC)

and survived the war after doing two of the set (operational) tours over Germany. As the war drew to a close I was training to teach history to returning students but before that could happen I was demobbed at Taunton as a married woman.

I loved my time in the ATS. As an only child it was a great change for me to have so much company – a lot of it so different from my own upbringing.

Moreen's watch sergeant, Margaret, on Douglas, Isle of Man. Courtesy of M. Moss.

As ever, friendships lasted and Moreen keeps in touch with a couple of old colleagues.

Moreen Head (later Moss) and friend Mary Vale – often taken for twins. Courtesy of M. Moss.

Anne's Story

Anne Walker (née Gillieson) joined the ATS in Edinburgh in 1943, when she was seventeen and a half years old. Her one-month basic training was done at Glencorse Barracks, where her results in the standard selection tests earmarked her for the Royal Corps of Signals and Intelligence Corps Y Service.

That meant six months' intensive training at the centre on the Isle of Man, including high-speed Morse training. At the end of this some ATS members of the course went to Harrogate in Yorkshire to work at Forest Moor intercept station and others, including Anne, went to Beaumanor near Leicester.

Initially she worked on the intercept of German communications. After victory was declared in Europe in 1945, the operators received extra training for the intercept of Japanese messages.

Life for Anne and some of her colleagues at Beaumanor turned out to be quite an experience. First of all there was the accommodation

– a cold, damp house in the nearby village of Quorn. Fortunately the lives of the ATS girls who'd been allocated this dismal billet were greatly improved by the kindness of their civilian neighbours. Anne remembers being given the key to a neighbouring house where the owners let her 'rest in a comfortable armchair', have a decent warm bath and hair wash, and keep some civilian clothes for off-duty hours.

The next billet was a slight improvement, although a very familiar one to ATS girls – a Nissen hut in the nearby village of Woodhouse Eves. 'Freezing cold and very difficult to get much warmth from the little round stove in the middle.'

Despite the vital importance of the work, on first reflection Anne found the life quite dull – being transported to and from their work-place and working difficult, but not unusual, shifts. Every twenty-four hours had three shifts averaging eight hours and this pattern ran for three or four days, followed by a day off.

Then she remembered that, although there were obviously peri-ods between shifts to allow for sleep, 'we were young, full of energy and silly so we probably didn't rest as much as we should have done.' There were unexpected happy occurrences.

With forty-eight-hour passes, Anne and some of her friends hitch-hiked to London on civilian lorries. Again, Anne remembers the kindness of the drivers. They used to make a regular stop at a transport cafe on the outskirts of London where they treated the ATS girls to a hot breakfast (despite rationing) – a real treat!

Anne had her first introduction to classical orchestral music at the De Montfort Hall in Leicester. She went to a concert given by Sir John Barbirolli with the Halle Orchestra, which he had only taken over as conductor in 1943. 'I was captivated by the music,' she recalls. An enthusiasm that has remained throughout her life.

Then there was the day in September 1944 when they went out into the village and found themselves in the midst of part of the American 82nd Airborne Division. The significance of this for the ATS involved nylons, cigarettes and that staple of ATS life – regular dances.

The important aspect of this for history was that these troops were assembling at points around the country waiting to be transported to east of England airfields to leave on Operation Market Garden. For them this was the airborne drop on Nazi-occupied Holland at the Nijmegen Bridge, ahead of the Allies' armoured push up to Arnhem – the famous 'Bridge too Far'. Although the Nijmegen Bridge was eventually taken from the Germans, there were many American casualties and, later in her life, Anne did visit the memorials at Nijmegen to bring back memories of Beaumanor.

The De Montfort Hall in Leicester was a venue that provided a great deal of entertainment for military personnel. One event there was, unfortunately, not really part of Anne's story – as she recalls with regret. Glen Miller and his American Band of the Allied Expeditionary Force gave a concert for these men of the 82nd Airborne Division, as he did in all areas where US troops were stationed in the latter half of 1944, until his death over the Channel on 15 December.

Naturally everyone tried very hard to get a ticket but not even the wiles of the ATS were enough to achieve this – the hall was filled to capacity with Americans. The concert was very low key and not reported in the local press. This situation was similar in a way to the earlier build-up of troops and equipment for D-Day. The numbers involved were such that the public knew something was going on, but not what, where or when.

The last few months of Anne's ATS career saw her on the move after she had asked to leave Beaumanor, where the intensive work on shifts was becoming a bit of a problem. Obligingly they did move her, as she says, from a 'select Signals group to the RAOC Depot at Chilwell which, at its peak, housed 3,500 ATS'. Not only that, as a corporal they put her in charge of a clerical office where she was lost, with no idea of what the girls, or she, were supposed to be doing. She discussed it with 'a very kind ATS officer' who learnt that Anne's ambition in civilian life was to work in a medical discipline and sent her off to the Peel Street Women's Hospital in nearby Nottingham. Anne was only a helper on the wards, which involved a lot of work with bedpans, compensated for by her having her own room in the Nurse's Home. She took advantage of the army career grants scheme for those about to leave the service and went to train in the Physiotherapy School at the Edinburgh Royal Infirmary. A satisfactory ending to her ATS years.

Six

Alongside the Royal Army Ordnance Corps

Stores, Storage and Shipments

Thousands of ATS girls worked in the vast depots of the Royal Army Ordnance Corps (RAOC). This was 'logistics' in a big way.

The RAOC operated major Central Ordnance Depots (COD), some of which were still being built during the war as demand grew. ATS were employed at all these depots, including:

- ◆ Branston (Clothing)
- ◆ Bicester (A new COD built during the war for a mix of stores)
- ◆ Chilwell (Motor Transport and spares)
- ◆ Didcot (General Stores)
- ◆ Donnington (Built during the war for technical stores)
- ◆ Feltham (MT spares)
- ◆ Greenford (Armament, engineer, signal and radar stores)
- ◆ Weedon (Small arms and machine guns)

Central Ammunition Depots (CAD) were at

- ◆ Bramley
- ◆ Corsham
- ◆ Kineton
- ◆ Longtown
- ◆ Nesscliffe

These, together with their hundreds of sub-depots, were the huge warehouses that held clothing, vehicles, vehicle spares, technical stores, general stores and ammunition.

Work involved the processing of thousands of receipt and issue vouchers. In today's computerised environment that might seem mundane and tedious but in wartime it was absolutely vital work and very labour intensive.

These depots kept the British Army moving, fighting and re-equipping throughout the war, in all operational zones. There were even several 'trial runs' in the lead-up to D-Day in 1944 to check the speed of delivery of supplies to the 21st Army Group. During this period, although the details were kept secret, all the ATS girls employed in Britain sensed that something 'big' was being planned. Everyone was working flat out and under pressure – none more so than the ATS serving with RAOC. In most RAOC depots all leave was cancelled.

They weren't just issuing stores against indents; they were making up what were known as Beach Maintenance Packs for use by troops after the D-Day landings. Each pack had to have the correct type and number of spares and parts; some had to be waterproofed. It was reckoned that between D-Day (6 June 1944) and the end of February 1945 the amount of supplies shipped across the Channel and handled by RAOC installations amounted to: 419,000 tons of ordnance stores, including millions of spare parts; 826,000 tons of ammunition; 10,000 fighting vehicles; 53,000 non-fighting vehicles. No wonder the RAOC welcomed its ATS girls!

It wasn't just hardware that kept the troops fighting. All corps and units had their own contribution to make towards keeping morale high. Commanders considered this to be a vital aspect of war. RAOC met an additional need in helping with this task – they supplied replacement clothing and toothpaste.

Brigadier A.H. Fernyhough CBE MC in his *History of the Royal Army Ordnance Corps 1920–1945* is very complimentary about the contribution made by the ATS to the functioning of the corps, as were several other senior officers. At the end of the war Major General L.H. Williams, the Controller of Ordnance Services, talked of 'steadfast loyalty and cheerful devotion to duty'.

RAOC Training

The RAOC provided training facilities for ATS members who were employed in their depots. A branch of the RAOC School was dedicated to the technical training of ATS girls before they were sent to ordnance depots. Specific training was carried out, for all troops, within the depots themselves, especially where tasks as varied as packing and waterproofing boxes or preparing armoured vehicles for overseas were involved. The RAOC Training Establishment, which had moved to the Leicester area in 1940, ran ATS ordnance officers' courses. These lasted for a month, covering the technical aspects of the ATS work in the depots.

Given the vital importance of all that was required of ATS members who worked in ordnance depots there was one type of specialist training that came as a bit of a shock to old military minds. Peter Birchall, in his comprehensive history of bomb disposal, *The Longest Walk*, talks of a 'strange phenomenon' during the Second World War – the emergence of ATS Ammunition Examiners (AE). In 1939 there were only about fifty trained male AEs in total in the army. Training times were shortened and intakes increased.

The ATS AEs trained for six weeks at the RAOC School of Ammunition which was part of CAD Bramley and were then posted, as required, to the CADs. They could expect to leave the completed course as lance corporals. The training, as described by Peter Birchall, covered the recognition, classification, composition, construction, functions and safe handling of all types of 'land service ammunition' – the official description of army ammunition to distinguish it from its naval equivalent.

ATS work in ammunition would be largely concerned with the three Rs – repair, reconditioning and re-packing. There could be several reasons why

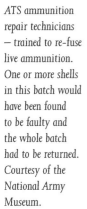

ATS ammunition repair technicians – trained to re-fuse live ammunition. One or more shells in this batch would have been found to be faulty and the whole batch had to be returned. Courtesy of the National Army Museum.

the three Rs were required; at this time ammunition could have suffered from water damage during the beach landings in France, or it could have been damaged in transit from the civilian munitions factories. This latter problem arose because ammunition was moved by rail from the factory to the ammunition depot and subject to 'loose shunting', i.e. the method of slowing or stopping the whole train was to let the wagons collide with each other. This was perfectly satisfactory for tightly packed and/or lighter contents but medium artillery shells could crash through another two wagons if shunted without being properly secured.

The ATS girls in the photograph (see p. 81) have been trained to re-fuse live ammunition. This consignment of shells might have been returned because the original fuse on one or two failed. The whole batch of shells would be returned to an ammunition repair workshop to have all the fuses changed. This was standard practice with batches of ammunition – one failure or miss-fire and the whole batch would be rejected and sent back to a CAD for examination.

Against this background the selection interview of ATS girls who wanted to undergo AE training would look for those who could organise teams to work methodically, didn't mind grease and dirt, had steady nerves and hands and strong arms. Qualities that are summed up concisely in the photograph!

Central Ammunition Depots

ATS girls worked in all the main RAOC ammunition depots. As described above, they went to CAD Bramley for training and could also have filled vacancies as clerks and typists on the permanent staff.

Corsham is remembered almost for one single reason: the storage and packing areas for ammunition had been built underground, using old quarries near Bath. The site spread over 148 acres and was divided into three sub-depots, one of which could accommodate eighty-five railway wagons for bulk shipment of ammunition.

The first ATS recruits arrived at CAD Kineton in October 1943 to cover driving, clerical and storage duties; those who had specialist AE training were also employed in the repair factories.

CAD Longtown covered a very large area about 15 miles outside Carlisle. It was reputedly difficult to recruit civilians during the war and by the middle of the war it was staffed by about 3,000 military, including an ATS Group. There was an ATS sub-district group at Carlisle.

COD Bicester

COD Bicester was purpose built during the war to meet the ever-increasing demands of the British Army. It held an assortment of stores and was earmarked as a supply base for when the Second Front opened. The area around the Oxfordshire market town of Bicester was chosen because of its ideal location for shipping MT and technical stores. It was in the south, fairly close to major ports on the west coast and had good rail and road links.

The initial plan was to have 1,700 ATS at Bicester, although this figure rose to nearly 3,000 before the end of the war. This meant that over 800 huts had to be built to accommodate them; then they were provided with an additional facility – their own railway station. This was close to the ATS camp and named Piddington. It already existed but wasn't used as a passenger halt. Initially the ATS were being driven to work 2 miles away, to the store sheds on the C site which handled MT items, using lorries that were very cramped with standing room only. As soon as somebody realised that this was very uneconomic in terms of lorries and fuel, adjustments were made to the Piddington platform and six railway coaches were obtained in 1943. They ran seven days a week to the halt at the C2 shed. Gradually ATS groups were moved by rail from other billets.

As E.R. Lawton and Major M.W. Sackett point out in their book, *The Bicester Military Railway* (BMR), the BMR was a significant feature of this new depot and the 'ATS trains' became a BMR institution.

COD Branston

ATS were employed at COD Branston, which was responsible for supplying all army clothing. And yes – if you are thinking that the name sounds familiar the depot was established in February 1938 in an old pickle factory near Burton-on-Trent! The storage requirements for clothing had outgrown the existing facilities in the Didcot ordnance depot and the Pimlico (London) clothing depot, and the new factory had 300,000 square feet of storage space. The statistics relating to quantities and storage requirements at Branston, together with the effect of events on the depot, emphasise the importance of clothing supply during wartime.

Brigadier Fernyhough records that when the army was mobilised hundreds of lorries blocked the roads for miles around the depot bringing their unit indents for clothing. Step forward the ATS! Twelve typists worked for days preparing lists and working out issue programmes for the storehouses according to the priority of each unit.

Then there was the replacement of uniforms destroyed on the retreat from Dunkirk and those lost from stores in France. Later there was the handling of clothing destined for Canadian and American forces; and, of course, as in all other army organisations, there was the build-up for D-Day.

A separate group had been formed to deal with clothing for the women's services. This was operated entirely by ATS girls and was 'extremely efficient' in Brigadier Fernyhough's words.

COD Chilwell

COD Chilwell had the largest contingent of RAOC/ATS; by 1945 there were 3,500 within the depot and another 5,000 spread around the sub-depots. ATS girls did the routine clerical and processing of stores work at Chilwell. It might have been routine but it was certainly vital work; troops in the war zones were dependent on the correct parts being dispatched to the right locations. Chilwell was also the HQ of the Army (RAOC) Vehicle Organisation which employed ATS girls. They worked on all the mechanised equipment that the depot issued to the British Army from tanks to motor-cycles; they collected vehicles from manufacturers and drove them around the country to units and ports; they processed and packed Motor Transport (MT) spares.

One item of equipment at Chilwell that was remembered by the many ATS girls who used them were the 'Lister trucks'. Originally designed to pull medium-weight loads around civilian factories, they were ideal for similar tasks in ordnance depots. They were built by the company of R.A. Lister, whose name was synonymous with the small town of Dursley in Gloucestershire. There, in 1867, they had started to manufacture agricultural equipment. The town's name usually appeared on all its engines alongside the company name. Even after decades, ex-ATS ladies like Betty Bateman identify their time at Chilwell by Lister-truck driving. Perhaps that's because the name lived on for the public in the shape of litter bins on high streets across the country – those galvanised steel bins surrounded by wooden uprights, the whole thing being fixed upright on the pavement by metal legs. Listers also manufactured generators that were used on RA gun battery sites.

Waterproofing of vehicles for beach landings was a dirty job and, when applied to something the size of a tank, involved climbing and balancing. There were two main requirements when all staff, including the ATS, were preparing tanks for overseas use: the vehicles must not fill up with water during beach landings; and the standard full maintenance schedule must be carried out before preservation so that when the preservatives were removed at the final destination the vehicles were ready to go. Lastly, the hatches were sealed and clipped down and the gun barrels were sealed off at the muzzle.

Betty was moved from the Chilwell site to their vehicle reserve depot at Handforth, south of Manchester and close to Wilmslow. Tanks were stored here and ATS girls helped to prepare them for overseas shipment.

In January 1944 Dame Leslie Whateley visited the 3,000 ATS girls who were working at Chilwell. She commented on what she saw as the 'monotonous but vital work of assembling and packing millions of spare parts'. She was aware of the reputation it had had in 1939, when ATS girls were first posted in, and for some time afterwards. ATS officer Margaret Sherman caught the essence of this reputation in her book *No Time for Tears* (In the ATS), published in 1944 and dedicated to 'The Camp on the Hill', as the barracks were known. Following her training at OCTU she says:

> Mary and I heard with a good deal of dismay that we were going to a Central Ordnance Depot somewhere in Northern England. 'Perhaps it won't be for longer than the initial three months,' Mary said comfortingly. 'Ordnance, who'd want that?' I said, with the nightmare vision of millions of issue and receipt vouchers. I didn't know then that the only thing I'd hate about Ordnance would be leaving it.

By the time of her visit, Dame Leslie thought that things had changed for the better. She put this improvement down to the work of Dame Regina Evans when she had been the commanding officer there.

Day One at Chilwell

Jean Atton arrived at COD Chilwell on the day that war was declared and served on in the ATS for a further eight years, reaching the rank of WO11 as a staff quartermaster sergeant (SQMS).

She worked in administration at Chilwell. Off-duty activities included ice skating in Nottingham and Sunday evenings at Beeston Chapel for hymn singing and supper.

Eventually, as an admin sergeant and with one ATS officer, Jean took forty ATS girls from Chilwell to the Leicester village of Wigston, where they were billeted in private houses in Station Road. One of her duties was to pay not only the girls but all the suppliers of property, billets, goods and services to the army units stationed in the area. And there were quite a few of them! Troops lived in private accommodation, in the Wigston council offices, above the police station and above the local pub.

The ATS girls were taken into Leicester by truck to work in a requisitioned factory where they applied a version of 'talcum powder' to the rubber inner tubes of bicycle tyres before they were packed together for dispatch to whatever units needed them. This prevented them from sticking together and damaging the rubber.

Jean applied for an overseas posting, which meant Belgium and Holland. In Brussels she remembers workers once again making lace – an interesting connection with the similar industry in Nottingham. Jean completed her ATS service in Germany at HQ BAOR.

Didcot

One of the age-old problems of stores handling is ensuring that what is physically on the shelves agrees with what the stock books say.

Before the war Didcot had been heavily involved in researching and developing machine accounting systems, including one that will be familiar to anyone who worked in RAOC depot receipt and issue departments: the Hollerith Punched Card system. Didcot also developed and used special packaging techniques.

By 1943 there were 850 ATS girls at Didcot and a camp had been constructed for them in Station Road. There was a photographic laboratory which had transferred from Aldershot in 1942. ATS girls were employed in this unit, which produced photographs and slides for RAOC training purposes. So it's possible that ATS members produced training material here that would be shown to RAOC ATS working in other depots.

Donnington

The central ordnance depot at Donnington was little more than an open site in the late thirties, but it was developed very rapidly as the demand for RAOC storage facilities grew. The depot handled signals and wireless stores, artillery equipment and stores, and engineering and radar items.

As the war progressed stores were transferred from the depot at Woolwich which, being close to London, became vulnerable to bombing. Like all other depots, units and regiments, the pressure increased even more as soon as D-Day was planned.

ATS Life at Donnington

As the initial organisation of Donnington involved building work – both for stores and accommodation – and the erection of the ubiquitous Nissen huts there was a lot of mud around. One ex-ATS lady who remembers all that mud (and the extra shoe-cleaning it caused) is Win Cook, who served between 1942 and 1946.

Win had a rather upsetting start to her ATS career, although it provided an excellent example of civilian life in wartime Britain. She joined in the south-west of England and had to travel to the training centre in Guildford. Win recalls her mother using precious rations of butter and bread to make sandwiches for her to eat on the train journey to the centre and explains what then happened:

> I was feeling so nervous about this unknown future that I couldn't eat them. I was alone in the carriage so I pushed them under the seat. I felt guilty over that for a long time afterwards. It was an offence to waste food, punishable by prison. My Mother never did find out!

After all that, Win found the Guildford training centre to be 'perfect' and not at all what she had expected.

After basic training she, and several other girls, were posted to Donnington in Shropshire. Win and her friends, like so many other ATS girls, found themselves faced with a very slow train journey taking all day because, in wartime, passenger trains were often shunted into a side line to allow troop trains or ammunition trains to go through. So this ATS contingent left London at 0930 hours and arrived at their destination at about 1800 hours. Win reminds us that, during the war, British clocks were two hours ahead – on double British Summertime. When they arrived, however, it was dark and raining; just the weather for a march to their camp! They were given a meal and buckets of tea. As Win says 'we just dipped our mugs in, no thought of hygiene then'.

She describes their living conditions:

> We were housed in tin huts, six bunk beds and a stove, and were not allowed to light a fire before 1800 hours. One small bucket of coal per hut. It was freezing. We were lucky in a way though. The rail tracks were alongside our line of huts. The trains often stopped there before going into the Depot and a kind-hearted driver would throw us a few large pieces of coal.

Marching to and from work in the winter months meant that lanterns were needed, as there were no street lights. So the outside girl of the front three carried the white light while the outside girl of the back three carried the red light. This 'lantern routine' had been instigated earlier, after a truck had run into a squad of marching troops, and it continued well into the fifties.

Things did get better for the girls, probably with the weather. Perhaps with the exception that once a week they were marched along the road for about a mile wearing their respirators. In the hot weather the smell of rubber was horrible, Win recalls, but she could see that it amused the local children.

She found, as did many ATS girls, that the majority of civilians were very good to members of the forces, inviting them into their homes. She reckons that they 'must have drunk endless cups of cocoa on visits to civilian friends. Tea was rationed of course, coffee – the bottled variety – was difficult to get'.

There were hundreds of civilians employed in the depot, many of whom came from Woolwich when the stores were transferred. There was a shortage of housing but both military and civilian authorities worked together, with help from the Ministry of Labour, to build around 1,500 properties.

Within the depot Win worked in one of the huge offices that dealt with the processing of stores vouchers; other ATS girls, who worked in the stores and amongst the tanks and guns, were often able to smuggle out bits of wood for their fires. It was not unknown, Win reveals, for someone to come back with a piece of wood pushed up the left sleeve of her greatcoat.

The Remaining CODS

COD Feltham

In 1942, following reorganisation, this depot became responsible for supplying vehicle spares to the army. The arrival of an ATS group enabled the depot to operate a double-shift system.

Greenford Depot

On the outskirts of London this depot eventually handled 75 per cent of the issues of technical stores. As soon as accommodation could be built the ATS arrived and their number peaked at 2,000. The British 21st Army Group, when in action in Western Europe, flew its supply indents to Northolt aerodrome. ATS dispatch riders (Don Rs) met the planes and brought the indents to Greenford in seven minutes. There they were sorted into the various depots that would issue the items if they weren't at Greenford itself and Don Rs would take them on to the appropriate location.

Weedon Depot

In Northamptonshire was the small arms depot that received the rifles sent by the United States under the Lend Lease scheme. ATS members helped in this activity.

Field Stores

This was really a historic, self-explanatory title, superseded by the concept of mobile ordnance field parks, which carried stores designed specifically to match the needs of the division that they were supporting, usually either armoured or infantry.

An exception to this were the field stores at Aldershot which, being the 'home of the British Army', was in large part a static base. The stores carried mainly furniture and furnishings for all the Aldershot barracks and married quarters. It would hold regular ordnance stores for units coming through in transit or being formed or re-formed.

In September 1939 King George VI – who continued as Colonel-in-Chief of RAOC after his accession – visited Aldershot. The Bedford section of the ATS was on parade there, acknowledged as doing 'good work' in the field stores.

In some kind of slip, Freudian or otherwise, in the reporting of those who were presented to the king at the event the male officers were identified by name in the *RAOC Gazette* but the ATS had only an 'Officer Commanding'.

Seven

The ATS on Wheels

The Women's Legion and the FANY had provided Motor Transport and Motor Driver companies both before and after the formation of the ATS. After September 1938, however, and certainly after 1940, all drivers were trained and worked as members of the ATS.

An ATS driving convoy ready to leave. Pictured is Sergeant Sheilah Clarkson, who was a young South African volunteer. Courtesy of the National Army Museum.

Perhaps the most famous ATS member to train as a driver was Princess Elizabeth (now Queen Elizabeth II). Her father King George VI, who took a great interest in her activities, was probably the envy of many fathers who themselves had been through the fraught experience of having to teach their own daughters to drive.

All locations that received, prepared, maintained and equipped vehicles, like the big RAOC depots and their sub-depots, had ATS drivers. They collected vehicles from manufacturers, took them to army depots for preparation and temporary storage, then drove them in convoys, often long distances, either to units or to the ports for overseas shipments.

Driving vehicles in convoy was recognised as being one of the most difficult jobs. Vehicle maintenance training was essential to cope with any breakdowns in the middle of a convoy, especially those hastening to deliver the vehicles to a ship within a tight time frame.

RASC Transport companies employed ATS drivers and dispatch riders; medical units had ATS ambulance drivers.

Driving at Chilwell

Cynthia Needham (née Thornton) remembers driving around Chilwell. She had tried to join up in Sheffield when she was seventeen and a half but was rejected because she was a nursing student in an isolation hospital, i.e. a reserved occupation. However, using a bit of initiative was the basis of life for many ATS girls so Cynthia left her nursing job to work in an office of the Food Ministry, thus re-classifying herself as a clerk and being accepted by the ATS just before her eighteenth birthday in 1943. Her basic training was done at Catterick Camp in Yorkshire, with further Motor Transport (MT) training at Fulford Barracks in York.

From there Cynthia went to the MT Section at COD Chilwell where she was billeted in Crusader Camp.

The depot was working on the build-up for D-Day. Cynthia drove an assortment of vehicles including Listers and Scammels; she was working between Buildings 157 and 201. Building 157 was a typical, huge parts shed, one of many employing ATS girls, where items were selected and packed ready for transit. Drivers, including Cynthia, then took the consignments to the railway sidings within Building 201, as Cynthia remembers it. These sheds had very large doors so that the railway wagons could be

One of the ATS companies, Chilwell Company at Crusader Camp, Chilwell, 1945. Cynthia Needham (née Thornton) is sitting in the first row on the right. Courtesy of C. Needham.

Cynthia Needham's group at Fulford Barracks, York, for MT training, she is on the front row, second on the left. The other girls are: Betty Russel, Elsie Warburton, Eve Worthington, Joan Halliday and F.W. Ward. The photograph was taken in 1943. Courtesy of C. Needham.

brought in at about 3 feet below the level of the shed floor. This meant that the floor of the railway wagon would be level with the floor of the shed, making it easy to move the loads straight into the wagon to be sent overseas.

Above left: Cynthia Needham (née Thornton) wearing her field service cap. Courtesy of C. Needham.

Above right: Cynthia Needham. Courtesy of C. Needham.

Cynthia Needham (née Thornton) with her future husband, Charles Chilwell. He's wearing an early version of the RAOC badge. Courtesy of C. Needham.

Driving Anything, Anywhere

Gwyneth Friday (née Oughton) was a young comptometer operator in civilian life. Her job was classified as an exempt occupation so she hadn't been conscripted. Instead she enlisted late in the ATS, in 1945, following a family dispute. As she admits, she just went off in what we would now call a 'hissy fit' and signed on. A comptometer operator was actually a specified ATS trade which should have been an indication of future postings but Gwyneth wasn't having any of that. All she wanted to do was to be a driver. She had signed on in Middlesbrough and went down to Glen Parva Barracks in Leicester for basic training. Then she went back to the Eaglescliffe Aircraft Recycling Plant run by the Air Ministry as a progress clerk; but with her one-track ambition Gwyneth had taught herself to drive and she ended up driving vehicles around the plant. This eventually got her to the post-war transit area in the Hook of Holland where she drove anything that was asked of her – staff cars for VIPs who travelled from the Hook up to Nijmegen, ambulances and 3-ton trucks. An interesting period followed at the HQ of the 21st Army Group – then the largest British Army base – at Bad Oeynhausen. One day she was asked to drive a sealed lorry, with outriders, to a large incinerator. She was told that it contained currency but not what type! It could have been German money that was no longer legal tender, as the Reichsmark had been replaced by the Deutschmark, or counterfeit money of any description because there had been a large black market in counterfeit notes, apparently a much larger operation than the Allies had originally thought. ATS women were reputed to have taken part in this activity. It could also have been counterfeit British sterling notes; large quantities of these were reputed to have been printed in Germany on Hitler's orders, to be dropped over Britain to destabilise the currency. A lot of possibilities there – too many for Gwyneth to guess the correct one.

In 1947, the year of the bad winter in Britain, Gwyneth was stationed in York which was very badly flooded. Water supplies had been cut off and Gwyneth found herself driving a water tanker round residential streets, dishing out the permitted quantity of water per household – similar to coal supplies for Nissen hut accommodation, one bucketful. She saw that as another opportunity for ATS initiative – until an eagle-eyed sergeant spotted that her mileage was higher than anyone else's on these runs and she therefore used more petrol and refilled her tanker more times than the others did. In reply she told the sergeant to go home and ask his wife if she could manage her family and household on one bucket a day! Bravery as well as initiative – which was lost to the service when Gwyneth left the ATS in 1948.

The Discipline of Driving

Sybil Worledge was one of the last girls to be actually conscripted into the ATS in 1944/45. She went to Pontefract in Yorkshire for her basic training and remembers the 'Bevin Boys' from the local mines hanging around the gates, looking for dates.

Sybil was selected for driver training and was posted to No. 1 Motor Transport (MT) training centre in Camberley, Surrey. This training centre, with its ATS sergeant instructors, had earlier had a famous 'recruit' – the then Princess Elizabeth. Aged eighteen, she had done a short course in driving and vehicle maintenance.

The ATS course was comprehensive, covering driving all kinds of vehicles from staff cars to 15cwt lorries and K2 ambulances. Maintenance and emergency repairs were extremely important, especially for ATS convoy drivers

Sybil Worledge, Horsley Hall, Gresford, N. Wales, when serving as a driving instructor. Courtesy of S. Worledge.

who were heading for ports or units ready for embarkation. Classroom work included map reading, although this must have been something of an acquired art for drivers out on the roads overnight in the pitch dark and with all signposts removed under wartime emergency regulations.

Sybil was in Cambridge for VJ Day – the final end of the war in Japan. Then on to Colchester and Bedford. The war might have been over and the winter mornings icy cold, but that was no excuse for missing the regular PT sessions down by the river.

Stories from other drivers tell of the discipline imposed around obedience to all maintenance and vehicle-handling regulations. Sybil was well aware of all the actions that are scarcely known today – like having to drain the radiator on cold winter nights because there was no anti-freeze available; she also reports that 'When we left our vehicles we had to remove the rotor arm from the distributor head – for safety – we had no keys in those days – only a press-button – or crank it!' She did get caught, however, and she was 'Confined to Barracks' (CB) for not doing an oil change on time. That meant fourteen days without a weekend pass and cleaning toilets and peeling vast amounts of potatoes when off duty.

Around this time she did a long run at night out to an airfield with no signposts and the colonel she was taking did the map reading. When they arrived in the middle of the night the officer pointed her in the direction of

On parade at Horsley, waiting for students to fall in. Courtesy of S. Worledge.

the cookhouse for a greasy ham sandwich which 'didn't go down very well at 0300 hours – but he meant well'.

As Sybil relates, 'I tried to peep through the door to see what was going on. All I could see was men helping each other along and in a very poor way. I think they must have been repatriated prisoners-of-war.'

There were happy memories of the Bedford Corn Exchange, where she met up with her WAAF sister for Saturday night dances and Sunday night sing-songs.

Sybil went on to Horsley Hall, in Gresford near Wrexham in North Wales, as a driving instructor. She trained the ATS and the WRENS there.

There was one regular event that she wasn't too keen on. As she says:

> Being duty driver was a bit frightening for me – having to meet the last train into Chester in a 2-ton lorry to bring people back to camp. There was no 'over the limit' then. Wrexham was teetotal on Sundays so everyone was drawn to Chester and as we drove on the main Wrexham to Chester road it was a bit scary.

Sybil thought that the food at Gresford was dreadful. Even the beloved tea urn had been used for soup earlier in the day. If parents sent anything that they could spare from their own food rations the girls would share it amongst themselves on their Tuesday 'night-in' for stitching and mending, as Sybil describes it.

Their ration of coal was one bucket a day, which didn't have much effect in a tin Nissen hut – especially when some heat was needed to stop the water in the showers and latrines from freezing. So the one bucket had to be matched by the usual ATS initiative – in this case 'borrowing' from the back of the cookhouse.

Sybil herself on driving instructors' maintenance day at Gresford with a K2 ambulance. Courtesy of S. Worledge.

Sybil's friend Jean with 15cwt truck at Horsley Hall, Gresford. Courtesy of S.Worledge.

Strange as it may seem, there were dock strikes during the war and the army took over their work. Sybil and other ATS drivers remember taking over duties to help keep the docks open.

All those adventures for a shilling a day but, as Sybil recalls, 'The comradeship was wonderful.'

Driving an Ambulance

Blanche Hamer (née Taylor) was a secretary in an agricultural builder's merchant when war broke out, but her job was classified as a reserved occupation so she couldn't volunteer for the ATS at that stage. In 1943 she managed to get her release from the job and enlisted. At one of her initial interviews her ATS fate was sealed. She told them that she had been driving her own car – a Standard 9 – since 1936. After her basic training she was sent for a driving test and then on to the driving section of an RAMC unit based in Keynsham, between Bristol and Bath. She actually stayed there until her demob in spring 1947.

Blanche was billeted in a house in a rural area where the food was good and she found life easy. Most of her duties involved taking doctors and

Blanche Hamer (née Taylor) with her ambulance outside her billet. Courtesy of R. Hamer.

Platoon of drivers at Keynsham. Blanche Hamer is second right on the back row. Courtesy of R. Hamer.

A 'sensible' photo of Blanche and her friends; her close friend Beryl is on the right. Courtesy of R. Hamer.

A 'not-so-sensible' grouping! The friendships ATS girls formed often remained with them long after the war was over. Courtesy of R. Hamer.

patients to Plymouth Hospital across the moors in all weathers, at any time of the day or night and in any type of vehicle that they requested, but mainly ambulances. She recounted how the smallest consignment with which she ever crossed the moors from Bath to Plymouth was a soldier's sample that had to be tested urgently in the hospital.

Blanche died in March 2004 and her memory is kept alive by her husband Roger.

Driving an Ambulance and Other Vehicles

Kath Gerrard (née Edwards) served with the ATS from 1941 until 1946, as a driver.

Driver training started in Aldershot. The memory that stays with Kath is that of learning to drive lorries with 'crash gears'. This was the old gear-box technology that preceded synchronised gear-changing; it required a higher standard of driving skill because the engine speed had to be adjusted when changing gears. Not quite the same thing, but reminiscent of another early

Kath Gerrard (née Edwards) on the right.
Courtesy of K. Gerrard.

driving technique involving gear changes on some military vehicles – that of double de-clutching.

Kath continued her MT training in Chester, taking field ambulances across to Parkgate on the Wirral to have the batteries charged.

Then it was off to Alton Towers, which was a very different environment to that of today. The property had been requisitioned by the War Office for use as a cadet training centre. Kath was still driving ambulances but, as she says, 'I was lucky as I could walk round the lovely gardens whenever I liked'. Her next posting, as a lance corporal, was to Kinmel Camp in North Wales. This was a very large camp built during the First World War, originally to provide a base for battalions raised in North Wales, although the Canadian and American armies also used it. It had its own Kinmel Camp railway which provided a connection with the main Holyhead line. This camp was always easy to spot on the old A55 North Wales route as it was opposite the famous white-marble church at Bodelwyddan.

Kinmel Hall itself was used as a hospital. Kath had a field ambulance, an American one and a small van in which to collect the rations for the hospital.

She completed her service in Shrewsbury as a full corporal, working mainly in the office but also in charge of a petrol pump – a great responsibility in those days.

Riding on Two Wheels

Brenda Horness (née Varty) joined the ATS in January 1943 in Middlesbrough and was sent for recruit training to St Ethelburga's School in Harrogate. There she experienced all the common trials and tribulations of basic training plus

Private Brenda Varty. Courtesy of B. Horness.

lots of laughs and singing of songs with 'odd words'. Scope for the imagination there!

When it came to choosing a future job Brenda opted for dispatch rider, which led to an interesting selection test. As Brenda recalls:

I was sent into a room where a senior officer was sitting behind a table on which was a small Meccano construction, a screwdriver and spanners. I was told to dismantle it, which I did, then sat back thinking that I had finished but – surprise – I was to rebuild it. This I managed to do. I suppose it was to see if I could use tools. I also had an eye-test and was issued with steel-framed spectacles for distance. These had flat-sided arms so as not to allow gas to penetrate when wearing a gas mask.

Having proved herself with the Meccano, Brenda found herself, with seven other ATS trainees, at the No. 1 Motor Transport (MT) training centre at Camberley in Surrey. This brought an issue of special kit – trousers, boiler suit, crash helmet, brown boots, three pairs of grey socks, a leather jerkin and a pair of gleaming yellow gauntlets. This rare burst of colour was designed for visibility when riders were hand-signalling or directing traffic when marshalling a convoy of vehicles.

They started training on Royal Enfield 250cc bikes, riding them round a field, and finished by being followed on an open road by a staff car carrying an observing officer. In between they'd done bike maintenance, rough off-road riding, map reading, drill and PT. Later, on public roads, they joined up with ATS girls who had been training on ambulances and utility vehicles and took over as outriders for the convoy, holding up civilian traffic at junctions and roundabouts so that the convoy drivers could practice keeping their vehicles together as would be required of them all in 'real life'.

Betty, and all her colleagues, passed the course. She could now wear a badge on her left arm with the letters DR over a pair of wings, and her chinstrap over the top of her issue cap instead of round the front. She was now a Don R, as all dispatch riders were called. With four ATS colleagues she went to 913 Coy RASC AAC (M) Transport based at Blundellsands, north of Liverpool. After a few days she was on her way, on detachment, to Preston as Don R for the lieutenant colonel commanding RASC in 4 AA Group. The ATS billet was a large terraced house at 74 Westcliff.

Betty signed for a 350cc Ariel bike from the RASC Don R she was replacing. He was off to 912 Coy RASC at Tamworth to await a move overseas. Assignments came in straightaway, including a nightly run with the mail to the railway station. As Brenda says:

> I was now working on my own and learning the hard way. No one at Camberley had told me how to ride on wet cobble stones or negotiate tramlines or to ride at night with the headlamp glass painted black with a small cross scraped off leaving just a glimmer of light showing to oncoming traffic.

Regulations and discipline applied to two wheels as well as to four – as Brenda found out on three occasions. Once she failed to immobilise her bike when leaving it for a few moments on the street while she went into a post office, on duty. She should have unscrewed the plug lead and taken it with her. The 'Red Caps' or the Military Police caught her. Beryl recounts that she was put on a charge but received no punishment. The officer said (jokingly) 'in future Pte Varty if you see any lurking MPs call them over and ask them to guard your motor cycle'.

The second occasion was when she was returning from a detail in Manchester on a Saturday morning. A few miles from the base everything went completely blank until she woke up on Sunday afternoon in Preston Royal Infirmary, before being moved to the military hospital at Winwick near Warrington. Mind you, a fractured skull and concussion was no reason not to have a military Court of Inquiry into her being in charge of a smashed motorcycle. 'I couldn't make a proper statement,' she explains, 'because I remembered nothing of the accident. But I was cleared of blame because the police had got witness statements saying the car had come from a minor road and I was on the major road.'

The third incident involved the theft of her Matchless 350cc bike from its place in the bike shed on camp. It was found on a local golf course. So that

From left to right: Nancy (a cook), Connie (canteen staff) and Brenda (Don R), 913 Company RASC, Transport, near Tamworth, Staffordshire, 1945. Courtesy of B. Horness.

meant another Court of Inquiry, with two officers brought in from elsewhere. Brenda was again cleared of the charge, this time because the bike had been parked within the bounds of a camp that was guarded twenty-four hours a day.

One incident highlighted the importance of the maintenance classes that all drivers and riders attended during training. Brenda was riding on duty

Private Varty (Brenda Horness) on a Matchless 350cc with 913 Company, RASC AAC (M) Transport, Drayton Manor, Staffordshire, 1945. Courtesy of B. Horness.

from Liverpool to Nottingham. At the highest part of the mountain pass in the Peak District her throttle cable snapped. The only signs of life around her were a few sheep who hadn't read any maintenance manuals. So Beryl got to work:

> I slipped the outer casing off the throttle, wrapped the inner wire round my gloved hand and gently levered it by resting my hand on my thigh. I limped down to civilization in bottom gear. There some soldiers directed me to a workshop where a fitter soldered the wire back into place.

This period of Brenda's service life was full of incidents, sport, entertainment, film shows interrupted by messages flashed on the screen recalling Brenda to camp for an emergency detail, leave cancelled for months before D-Day. In other words, just an ordinary life for an ATS Don R.

During this time she had met her husband, whom she married after he was demobbed in 1948. Brenda was demobbed in 1946 in York or, to give it its correct title, 'Military Dispersal Unit No. 2 York'. She describes her leaving presents as 'discharge book, ration card, clothing coupons, cash allowance draft to buy clothes, war gratuity payment, 56 days demob leave and many happy memories'.

The girls relaxing outside the hut at Chester. Courtesy of B. Horness.

'The tableaux', Catterick Garrison, 27 June 1992 – the Royal Signals Motorcycle Display Team, plus one ex-ATS girl, aged 69 – Brenda Horness (on top)! Courtesy of B. Horness.

Eight

The ATS Band (and Other Musical Talents)

There was much that kept the girls in khaki on the move, from determination to patriotism. Something that did it literally was the ATS band.

The ATS was a distinct service within the British Army and that was reason enough for it to have its own band. After all, military music dated back to the seventeenth century, when Cromwell's New Model Army was created with a stipulation that music would be provided. Trumpets for the cavalry, drums for the infantry; their purpose being to send communications to the troops – either on the battlefield or in camp, where musical summons were issued at reveille in early morning and last post at night, with various calls in between. The ATS band aspired to different duties, but the history of its rather short existence (1941–46) demonstrates how important it was for the image of the ATS.

The band was born at Norbury House, No. 14 Recruit training centre in Droitwich, Worcestershire. A young subaltern who was serving there – A.V. Stebbing (later Mrs Cobb) – called for musically inclined or, preferably, skilled members of the permanent staff to volunteer to form an ATS band. As was the way in military life, this meant that she instantly became the unofficial Director of Music. Eighteen volunteers stepped forward to form an unofficial drum and bugle band and the band master of the Worcestershire Regiment – WO1 George C. Bixley – lent a similarly unofficial hand in getting the group into shape.

Interestingly Brigadier Fernyhough, who was so complimentary about the achievements of the ATS attached to his own corps – RAOC – relates in his history of that corps that the RAOC band had been 'recognized but unauthorized' and struggled for many years; then it received official status at the end of 1938 – 'in view of the need to improve recruiting'. So the ATS band was not the only one to be important in tackling manpower shortages.

Very quickly the ATS band became popular, receiving requests to attend parades around the country. This gave rise to several administrative problems. In 1941 Junior Commander Stebbings took these matters to another junior commander, who was the ATS publicity officer at the War Office, based in Curzon Street in Mayfair. The publicity officer agreed to sort out three matters: insurance for the instruments, including cover for when they went on tour; the need for the group to be formally recognised through the usual military medium of having an authorised War Office 'establishment'; and the provision of funds for what were loosely described as necessities.

The band's HQ was moved to London, to No. 2 London District Transit Camp in Gower Street. (An address known to other ATS girls who worked there – mainly underground close to the tube line that served Gower Street underground station.)

Recruiting parades were important; sometimes they came under the title of 'Salute the Soldier' events, but all with the same purpose. A drill instructor from one of the guards regiments would give extra lessons for these occasions; lessons which were also given to any ATS squads specially selected to take part in recruiting parades.

The band received its official establishment, which increased over the years. First of all it was for sixteen members of a drum and bugle band. Lorna Smith was appointed as the drum major. Then it grew into a full brass band. Finally, in January 1944 the War Office Establishments Committee increased the number to fifty-five with the status of a full military band.

This number included Sergeant David Morris of the Welch Regiment, who had already helped to train the smaller group, and WO1 Band Master H.C.F. Monk ARCM of the 1st Battalion, the Essex Regiment.

Latterly a pipe band was included in the formation. They wore khaki jackets but were given permission to wear dark green Hunting Stewart kilts – perhaps because it would have been difficult to swirl in the ATS issue skirts that the rest of the band wore as part of their normal uniform.

As if any further proof was needed of its status, the ATS band followed the tradition of military bands and produced a dance-band section. Who has worn uniform and not danced to this special section of a regimental or corps band? The ATS dance band became well known and played at popular venues like the Queensbury All-Services Club at the London Casino in Old Compton Street, Soho.

All entertainment programmes that included a performance by the ATS military or dance band cited the standard expression that they appeared 'By kind permission of the Director ATS' – during the active life of the band this would be either Chief Controller Jean Knox or Chief Controller Leslie Whateley. The band also featured in radio programmes for the forces. The band marched and paraded in towns and cities from Cumbria to Cornwall. Then, at the end of the war, it toured overseas.

In June 1945 there was a performance at the Theatre des Champs Elysees Festival d'Amitie Franco-Britanique – the British Exhibition in Paris. In 1946 they sailed on the liner *New Hellas*, which left its berth on the Clyde with a group of Italian prisoners of war, who were being repatriated to Taranto in Italy. There the band played to 1,000 British troops who were waiting to return home. Afterwards the band sailed on to the Middle East. At the start of this tour they were based at the Allenby Barracks in Jerusalem, attached to 512 Company ATS. These barracks were named after Field Marshall Viscount Allenby, whose distinguished First World War career culminated in the defeat of the Turks in Palestine. The tour continued to the Middle East training centre in Gaza and to Mount Carmel in Haifa with 519 Company ATS.

Sadly the band ceased to exist after 1946 because most of its members were demobbed; but we shouldn't say goodbye to it without mentioning an

Last full photo of the ATS band. Courtesy of the National Army Museum.

earlier event that might resonate today – a football match held at Wembley Stadium (probably in 1944) between England and Scotland. The band of the Scots Guards played for Scotland. The 'Full Military Band and Pipers of the Auxiliary Territorial Service' marched and played for England.

From One Instrument to Another

Cath Hedley (née Heath) was a music teacher whose father refused to let her join the ATS in 1939 so she had to wait until she was twenty-one in 1941. She enlisted in Evesham and went to Durham for basic training. Selected for Ack-Ack duties she went to Oswestry in the very early days of this new employment for the ATS, learning to use the target location equipment.

Too early, perhaps, for the command sergeant major (CSM) disliked having to instruct women but eventually came round when he discovered that they were often easier to train than men. One memory that sticks in Cath's mind is of the large size of the receivers and transmitters used for communication across the battery sites, which made them difficult to adjust.

Unusually she remained at Oswestry, reaching the rank of corporal; but her main memory is of music! Once it was known that she was a competent piano player she was 'allowed' to play in the station band at unit dances – the only woman to do so.

The insignia that meant more than her corporal's stripes was the lyre that she was permitted to wear on her sleeve. This badge had been designed in the early years of the century to be worn by all ranks in a band. It consisted of a lyre, surmounted by a king's crown, within a half border of laurel leaves. The lyre was considered to be the most important classical instrument of ancient Greece – a plucked string instrument in a U-shaped frame.

More Music with the Guns

Dorothy Marsh (née Thompson) served from 1942 to 1946 with the RA as a predictor operator on radio location with 484 (M) HAA Battery; she served in France, Belgium and Germany, having been 'claimed' by her older sister Evelyn who was also an ATS Ack-Ack operator.

They both had another type of instrument when away from the gun sites. Dorothy played a bugle and Evelyn a kettle drum – and their battery had its own band. So they played with it on marches and in town centres, both at home and overseas.

There never seemed to be any shortage of amateur musicians and pianists in the army, who could make up groups and small bands or just start up a sing-song by sitting down at the nearest available piano. The reason for this lies in the way of life in the previous decade. There was little recorded music available, even after the arrival of the wind-up gramophone. In small market towns and villages residents provided much of their own entertainment, which required musicians of one sort or another. If there was access to a piano people learned to play it, either by ear or by sight from the abundant sheet music that was sold commercially. To accompany the piano there was often a fiddle, if not a violin, or a mouth organ, which was a popular, inexpensive source of entertainment.

Dancing

Few accounts of life in the ATS omit a mention of dances. In large camps there was always some drill hall or canteen large enough to provide a venue and they were not too difficult to arrange. They also offered an easy way of meeting up with the opposite sex in a familiar environment – bearing in mind that everyone had to wear uniform and there were limited opportunities for meeting young men locally, because they were also serving elsewhere in uniform. The film about the ATS, *The Gentle Sex*, has very descriptive scenes of a unit dance.

Some even danced to the Glen Miller Band, which performed live in various locations where there were American troops. The majority of the wartime big bands were American or Canadian. There were a few British RAF, Royal Marine and naval dance bands. For the thousands of ATS girls working in RAOC depots there was always the chance of listening or dancing to The Blue Rockets – officially the RAOC dance orchestra. It had been formed in 1941 and led by a well-known name in the music world, Eric Robinson. They played on BBC radio, including *Music While You Work* and, like the ATS band, on general forces programmes. As their popularity grew they started to make recordings as well. Despite all this, however, they weren't allowed to neglect their corps' responsibilities. They played at regimental dances and backed singers and soloists who performed in amateur shows put on in the ordnance depots.

Singing

The faculty of the ATS for song in any circumstances always amazes me.

So said Eileen Bigland in her book *Britain's Other Army*. She had noted that, even when doing dirty jobs involving anti-rust preservatives (as in an unspecified COD, but probably Chilwell), the girls were either whistling or singing. The ATS girls sorting letters and parcels in the Home Postal Centre in Nottingham also confirmed Eileen Bigland's view. Barbara Danter (née Miller) remembers working various shifts in the Vyella factory in Nottingham – one of the 100-plus buildings requisitioned for the Home Postal Centre. Freezing cold and with the doors wide open because lorries were arriving and leaving continuously twenty-four hours a day, singing kept them going but caused some concern amongst the supervisors, who worried that the musical endeavours might make the girls careless over sorting the mail into the correct pigeon holes. So they would come round from time to time, select a box at random and check that the letters had been correctly allocated. Perhaps they closed their ears to some of the songs, especially if they were senior NCOs. Still remembered today by ATS girls is:

> Around the corner and under a tree
> The Sergeant Major made love to me
> He kissed me once, he kissed me twice,
> He kissed me once again.
> And though it wasn't the thing to do
> He kissed me once again –
> Around the corner ...

More formal sing-songs often formed part of an evening's entertainment if there were no dances or shows to go to.

Nine

A Miscellany of Vital Activities

The answer to the question 'where did the ATS serve' must be anywhere and everywhere in Britain that they were needed to fulfil their designated role of releasing male soldiers to serve in the front line.

ATS duties with the four organisations where they were employed in large numbers, the Royal Artillery, the Corps of Royal Engineers, the Royal Corps of Signals and the Royal Army Ordnance Corps, have been described earlier.

There were many other trades, locations and corps that also needed the support of the ATS; in these roles the girls in khaki helped, in their different ways, to keep the British Army functioning. If pins were stuck into a map of Britain today to highlight all the locations where ATS served, whether singly or in their hundreds, the paper would probably end up being shredded by perforations.

With all the place names mentioned in wartime histories and diaries, we can see why local communities are still aware of sites that played a significant role during those war years. Sometimes there's a building that was requisitioned by the War Office during the war. There are several of these to be seen around Nottingham, including that at the Trent Bridge cricket ground. There are campsites that may have been redeveloped by a large company that acknowledges its historical context. The old barracks at Warley in Essex fall into this category, as described by Eileen Green in the story below of her 'different journey'. Sometimes there's just an area preserved with evidence of gun emplacements, as on the Great Orme in Llandudno, North Wales.

Towns that have laid out memorial gardens or, as it is called in Boston, Lincolnshire, the Veterans' Way, have plaques commemorating the ATS.

It's probably true to say that most ATS girls moved several times during their service years – not just from training depots to their permanent sites but from job to job as they were required by units to fill vacancies. Halfway through a morning's routine work an ATS girl might be called into an office and given a posting order and a railway warrant for the next day. Another day and another location on the 'ATS map' of the British Isles.

A Different Journey

Eileen Green (née Hansell) was born in Essex and her seven years of service saw her mainly in one location in that county; except for an unexpected journey that she made in the middle of her service.

As D-Day approached in 1944 areas in the south of England and along the east coast were filling up with vehicles, supplies and troops in preparation for that critical event. Eileen was an NCO in Warley Barracks in Essex which, as she recalls, was the only major barracks that had to be cleared of everything, including stores and administrative personnel to make room for D-Day formations. So Eileen found herself on a train heading for Blackpool on the Fylde Coast in north-west England or, more exactly, to Squires Gate camp in Lytham St Annes.

This was a holiday camp that had been requisitioned by the War Department for use as a primary training centre, i.e. a training centre for raw recruits – No. 13 Primary Training Centre. Eileen remembers the chalets in the camp which would, at a future date, become a Pontins holiday camp.

Wartime train journeys were never easy at the best of times. Rail traffic increased; some of the loads carried were so heavy that they slowed down the engines, some of which could manage only 14mph if pulling a dozen or more coaches up a gradient; civilian timetables were constantly altered; cuts had to be made to services during the coal shortage of 1941.

Eileen's train journey was, as she describes it, an administrative nightmare. So much to keep an eye on, and she tells the story of how slow it was because they kept being shunted into sidings to allow troop trains to come through. Then they stopped at various stations en route so that local units could provide them with haversack rations and drinks – known as keeping them fed and watered.

Warley Barracks officers' mess, 1943. This photograph includes: batmen, batwomen, cooks, waitresses, porters, civilians, messing officer and stewards. Pat Christie (ATS) is in the front row, third in from the left. Courtesy of G. Shadrack.

Eileen was involved in keeping records of everything that they took with them from the barracks, from stores to the names of all the ATS girls involved in the move. It was a massive effort for a relatively short period of time – two or three months – until the D-Day landings were completed and they could then move everything and everybody back to Warley. There was plenty of additional administration to be done by the ATS during their time at Squires Gate camp, including keeping records of male recruits who came for six weeks' basic training.

One interesting difference that Eileen noticed during her time on this section of the coast was that, unlike the southern areas, it was quiet, 'No risk of bombing' as she puts it. It was almost like a peacetime existence. She even had the impression that the authorities weren't so strict about blackout regulations.

Eileen had been an enthusiastic and uncomplaining recruit despite experiencing the 'teething troubles' of the early years of the ATS. She had tried to volunteer in 1938 but was turned away as being too young at seventeen years of age. She tried again in 1939 and signed up at Warley Barracks – home of the No. 1 Infantry Training Battalion. There was no accommodation for the women, who were billeted in private homes in the area, which

Warley Barracks, between 1939 and 1942. Eileen Green (née Hansell) is fourth left on the front row. Courtesy of G. Shadrack.

for Eileen meant her own home. There wasn't much in the way of uniform either. That arrived over months, bit by bit.

Basic training was done at Warley Barracks by TA staff – both men and ATS officers. The centre and the training itself were still not very well organised. Eileen's most lasting memory is of doing drill with male NCOs – a memory shared by hundreds of ATS who went through a similar experience. Drill arguably came as the greatest shock of military life for the majority. Stepping off on the correct foot, shoulders back, head up, keeping in step, changing step on the march, arms swinging to the correct height – all whilst trying to absorb the thundering instructions echoing across the parade ground. Then no sooner does the squad master all the intricacies of a perfect quick march than the taskmaster with the stripes on his or her arm wants it done all over again – as a slow march. Not quite as easy!

Warley had been a military area, particularly for training purposes, since the eighteenth century. In 1881 it became the depot for the Essex Regiment and in 1925 the garrison church became the official Essex Regiment Chapel. Over 1,000 men of the Essex Regiment died during the Second World War. Eileen was very grateful for the survival of one member of the regiment – the man she met at Warley who became her husband in 1942. During the war the barracks became the No. 1 Infantry Training Centre, where recruits of all infantry units came for six weeks' basic training. Eileen's husband was on the permanent staff.

The original gym buildings are remembered by Eileen for the dances that were held there during the war. By 1946 there were 300 ATS working in the barracks, as stores and administrative clerks and cooks. Married quarters that lined a nearby street were cleared to provide accommodation for the ATS so that, in turn, there was more room in the barracks for recruits.

Eileen enjoyed her work as a stores clerk; she went on to finish her service as a CSM, responsible for the 300 ATS girls at Warley. More than sixty years later she can even remember the numbers of the various forms that were used in the stores, particularly one called a 'hastener' which she sent to suppliers when stores weren't received on time.

Eileen remembers the periodic lectures laid on for them all by the Army Bureau of Current Affairs (ABCA) to keep them up to date with what was going on in military, civilian and political circles, as far as was permitted by the Official Secrets Act.

The last memory, as for hundreds of others, was the Victory Parade in London. They were trained in Bushy Park, north of London, by senior ranks in the guards and completed the 5-mile march without even noticing the distance.

With the post-war amalgamation of regiments and the shrinkage in army numbers, Warley Barracks was sold and is now occupied by the Ford Motor Company. With her and her late husband's connections to Warley Barracks, Eileen is happy with the recognition that Ford gives to the historical site.

Commemorating the ATS of Warley Barracks and Essex

The Essex Regiment Chapel still exists there and is used for regimental occasions; the old depot officers' mess became the Regimental Association's headquarters and one of the three original gyms remains.

In 2001, after a great deal of research and hard work, a plaque was installed in the chapel:

> To commemorate the service by women of the Auxiliary Territorial Service stationed at Warley Barracks and elsewhere in Essex during the Second World War. Presented by members of the Chelmsford Branch ATS/WRAC Association
> 4 March 2001

The branch secretary Gina Shadrack (whose story is told with that of the Royal Army Education Corps) managed to get the details of eighty-one ATS members who had served in Essex. The list demonstrated the range of occupations in the ATS – from Ack-Ack operators to ambulance drivers, from cooks to clerks, from telephonists to teleprinter operators.

Ann's Story

Ann Atkinson (née Spice) served for six years in the ATS as an orderly. This is one of those trades, like cooks and clerks, that sometimes get overlooked in the reckoning of the ATS contribution to the war effort. These girls, like Ann, kept the army fed and watered, well-turned out, comfortably housed and properly documented – in so far as any of that was possible in wartime.

Ann Atkinson (née Spice), 7 February 1947. Courtesy of A. Atkinson.

Together with her sister she enlisted in Kent; as was the way of these things her sister was sent to London for basic training while Ann went to Glen Parva Barracks in Leicester. She then went to work in the officers' mess in Budbrooke Barracks – the home of the Royal Warwickshire Regiment.

One day the staff were told that they would be looking after a Very Important Person who would be dining in the Mess with a group of about a dozen of his officers. Until the day arrived they didn't know who the visitor was going to be.

It was General Montgomery, who commanded the British Eighth Army at the Battle of Alamein. Ann was supervising in the dining room and the kitchen staff asked her to get the general's autograph, having brought in their autograph books in anticipation. The first problem was that none of the mess staff were allowed to speak to Montgomery directly. All comments were to be addressed to one of his officers. However, he did agree to sign the books; the one member of the mess staff who didn't get a much-prised signature was Ann herself because she had only a small diary not a proper autograph book, which wasn't acceptable for some unknown reason. She did carry a memory of the enormous limousine that the general and his entourage travelled in, though.

What Ann and some of her colleagues didn't understand was why General Montgomery had suddenly turned up at Budbrooke. In fact the reason or at least one of the reasons was quite simple. Montgomery had been commissioned into the Royal Warwickshire Regiment in September 1908. In December of that year he joined the 1st Battalion on the North-West Frontier in India.

The ATS contingent eventually left Budbrooke and Ann moved to COD Chilwell, where she worked in the ATS officers' mess. The photograph of Ann shows clearly the ATS shoulder badge. At the end of her service she travelled to York to be demobbed.

Paying the Bills

Betty Mitchell (née Ellis) throws an interesting light on reasons for joining the ATS together with reasons for supporting and publicising its existence and achievements during the following sixty years.

When Betty left school in the late thirties she worked as a cashier at Sainsbury's – a good job with a well-known company that she describes as 'very efficient'. When she raised the question of joining one of the women's services her father, like so many others, wasn't keen.

Service life wasn't seen as being suitable for young ladies but Betty saw it as an opportunity for young girls to show what they could do. The family discussions ended in the summer of 1940 after HRH Princess Mary, the Princess Royal, appealed on the radio for 10,000 women to join the ATS. Betty joined in her home town of Farnham, went to Reading for her medical and to Aldermaston in Berkshire for basic training.

Aldermaston – a familiar name to hundreds of ATS recruits – was a country house and grounds taken over by the War Office. The owners continued to live in part of the house while the remainder was occupied by the permanent staff of the training centre. Unsurprisingly, recruits (about sixty per regular intake) were housed in huts in the grounds. Such a familiar story!

There were eight beds to a hut and Betty loved it. She was an only child, her favourite books being stories about boarding schools, and she imagined a similarity. That may have been stretching the imagination a bit far because the hutted 'dormitories' actually had no toilets! That meant an early morning dash up to the house or a visit to a toilet provided by nature behind the nearby hedge. Betty was a hedge girl!

Thirteen recruits from Betty's intake were posted to Salisbury to work in the Southern Command Pay Office with the 6th Gloucestershire Regiment Clerical Company. For the first three weeks they were billeted in a theological college in the Cathedral Close. The college had toilets but the close had a very inconvenient gate which was locked every night before the girls returned from their evening entertainment in the town.

The next billet was a real boarding school for girls – the Godolphin School, founded in 1726 and still in existence today. The ATS girls paraded before work outside their billet and then marched to the office. Betty remembers that march – left wheel, right wheel and straight on down. They considered themselves to be much smarter than the male soldiers.

There's a tendency to associate pay offices with pay books and pay parades, but that's only half the story. Command pay offices like the ones in which Betty worked paid the army's bills. Not often recognised in wartime histories but one of the many backroom functions that were of great importance. As Betty recalls, there were two documents for every transaction: the invoice on a P1922 and the P1964 – a detailed copy of the invoice that had to be verified by an officer, often after a reminder.

There were payments for requisitioned land – all those ancestral estates and parkland for training or operational centres and storage of vehicles and ammunition. Payments for buildings – like those in Nottingham that were used by the Home Postal Centre. Payments that brought home to Betty the true cost of war in human terms, as well as material considerations, were those for re-clothing and re-equipping the soldiers who'd been evacuated from Dunkirk with damaged uniforms and without any personal equipment. Hundreds of payments, but all straightforward stuff for the efficient ATS pay clerks like Betty and her colleagues.

Just one type of invoice fooled Betty the first time she saw it – a payment for 'removal of night soil'. As she says, it was lucky that one of her friends was a country girl who explained the facts of life to her – night soil being human excrement collected at night from any toilets that had no water-flushing facility or from cesspits without treatment mechanisms. There were a lot of those in the hundreds of makeshift army camps around the country.

Betty served for two years during which time she married. She then left on compassionate grounds because her father died and her mother needed help in coping with her loss. Betty was already a sergeant.

Like other ATS veterans, Betty has worked very hard to keep the name of the ATS in the public eye, because she sees the formation and achievements of the service as a turning point in the emancipation of women in Britain. They did work thought to be impossible for women at that time and lifted the hopes and aspirations of so many women above their previous expectations. She also feels that the ATS veterans are often overlooked, perhaps because the title doesn't contain the word 'women' and it changed so dramatically in 1949 when the service was re-established as the Women's Royal Army Corps. In terms of historical background this compares unfavourably with the similar wartime/peacetime titles of the Women's Auxiliary Air Forces (WAAF) and the Women's Royal Air Force (WRAF).

Betty is amused by the way in which she is regarded by the very young members of her family. Even at primary school age they hear about the Second World War and are amazed that she was actually there as a soldier. This led her to write a poem about this generation gap, which was published locally, and is included in the Epilogue.

Esther's Story

Esther Pring (née Stone) joined the ATS in 1941 as a volunteer. She had her medical in Salisbury and went to Aldermaston for her basic training. Her story is a familiar one, and told in her own words:

> It was an experience getting off that train and seeing so many girls doing the same thing, all from different backgrounds. But once in our uniforms we were all the same, one big family, a lot were very homesick. But we all settled in and got to know each other over the weeks. After training we were all sent to different places
>
> I went to a place in Luton called Luton Hoo, a large stately house. We were in huts on the tree-lined drive and went each day to parts of the house and surroundings to work. Later in 1941 we came under military law. So now we were no longer called volunteers and we had the same ranks as the men. I became Private Stone.

Hut 32, Honiton. Esther Pring is in the centre. Courtesy of E. Pring.

Afterwards I was posted to Exeter. We lived in empty houses on the main road and worked at Higher Barracks each day. A lot of girls went to confirmation classes. I did and was confirmed in the Lady Chapel of Exeter Cathedral. My officer took me in her little sports car. I was confirmed by the Bishop of Crediton.

After a while I was posted to an ATS training camp – Heathfield Camp in Honiton, where we trained new recruit intakes. I got my first stripe – so I was now a L/Cpl. I had a nice group of recruits in my hut each time and we all mixed well. Lots of drill, lectures and discipline.

I met my future husband at the end of 1941. He was a medic stationed nearby. We were married on 15 November 1942. By December he was in North Africa then later in Italy.

I was sent on a Corporal's course at Whittington Barracks in Lichfield, Staffordshire. Then I went to Bovington Camp where I got my promotion to Corporal (Cpl). I took over the running of the ration stores for the ATS Company. When not at the stores I was the Admin Cpl working with our Company Sergeant Major (CSM). We got on very well and I enjoyed the work. We lived in a place called Higherwood in houses. We had a canteen where we could meet up in the evening; our medic could play the piano so we had many a good singsong. We had a hut in the camp that was our cinema with a tin roof that was very noisy when it was raining. There would be a dance now and again in the Garrison room. It was all great company.

The food was very plain but everyone was very healthy. We were very well looked after, with regular medicals.

When there was an air-raid we would huddle under the stairs. Bombs did drop on our surroundings; there was one that didn't go off so we NCOs had to take turns on guard duty until the bomb disposal squad made it safe.

There are so many things one remembers about those years. I wouldn't change a day of my time in the Forces and I will always remember the wonderful comradeship we had, and the girls I will never forget. We grew up fast and became independent. It taught us a lot. I am so grateful for those years and also that the ATS and other girls in the Forces helped pave the way for the girls serving today. They are doing a great job.

We proved that we were more capable than was thought possible. I was asked to stay on and take further promotion but my husband wanted me to come home and find us a place of our own – no such luck at that time. I left the ATS after the war in 1945.

Whittington Barracks, 1942, Lichfield, Course 13. Courtesy of E. Pring.

Royal Army Education Corps

The British Army had organised education for its troops since around 1846; by 1920 this branch was known as the Army Education Corps and in 1946 it became the Royal Army Education Corps.

During the war years the main problem for army personnel was getting a couple of hours a week off work to attend 'unit education' courses, which ended up being rather disjointed and not always successful.

Inevitably, the Army Education Corps turned its attention to the ATS and 1941 saw the appointment of the first ATS educational staff officer at the War Office. The Army Bureau of Current Affairs (ABCA) gave a well-remembered series of short lectures in units. ATS groups attended the lectures but, in the view of some education staff, the ATS were interested more in local and personal issues than in international affairs.

Illustrated is a copy of 'WAR', the pamphlet which ABCA produced on a fortnightly basis. The seven points on the back cover, giving examples of criticism, illustrate why ABCA lectures were not always welcome – although they did provide the chance of a sit-down for any girls who were on their feet all day.

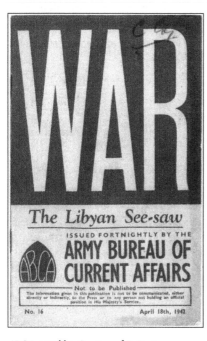

ABCA pamphlet. Courtesy of B. Danter.

The edition illustrated here is much treasured by ATS veterans because it contains an article explaining 'The Work of the ATS – the Army of Women in Khaki'. Although the report explained the basic organisation and work of the ATS, it devoted most of the space to a description of the growing use of suitable ATS members in mixed heavy anti-aircraft batteries of the RA and especially in searchlight units; or, as the ABCA described it, 'the most extraordinary development'.

There was concern about preparing all troops for civilian life after demobilisation – although this matter had been addressed before there was absolute certainty about the outcome of the war. To avoid the problems that had arisen with unit education it was deemed that courses which provided pre-release education should be residential. For this purpose the Army Education Corps established Army Formation Colleges (AFC) as part of what was known as the Release Period Education Scheme – a forerunner of what were later called Resettlement Courses. The AFCs were residential and for all ranks, male and female. The courses covered a comprehensive range of subjects:

- Science and Maths
- Commerce, including Banking and Accounting
- Modern Studies, including Languages and Politics
- Art and Architecture
- Trades, such as engineering and building
- Domestic Science, including childcare. (Here there was a slight slippage over equality issues in the army; this course was described as being of interest primarily to women, forgetting the Army Catering Corps, RAOC laundry and bath platoons, male orderlies and batmen. But we know what they meant!)

There were also courses for the instructors themselves to avoid the kind of mistakes listed in the 'WAR' pamphlet.

The AFCs were designed to cover the command areas in Britain and ATS girls were familiar with most of the colleges for one reason or another.

- No. 1 Scottish Command: Newbattle Abbey, Dalkeith, Midlothian. This became No. 1 AFC in 1945. Newbattle was the ancestral home of the marquesses of Lothian, with the site of the abbey itself dating back to the twelfth century. It was given to the nation in 1937 to be used as a civilian educational college but, like other similar estates, it was taken over by the War Office and used as the training centre for the Royal Army Medical Corps and the ATS. So Newbattle joined the list of large, requisitioned estates whose grounds suddenly sprouted the famous huts to accommodate all the military.

- ◆ No. 2 Northern Command: Welbeck Abbey, Worksop, Nottinghamshire. Welbeck was the ancestral home of the dukes of Portland. During the war the then duke and duchess retained half of the house for their own use and the remainder was given to the War Office.
- ◆ No. 3 Southern Command: Chiseldon Camp, Wiltshire. This was a hutted camp.
- ◆ No. 5 Eastern Command: Luton Hoo, Luton, Bedfordshire.
- ◆ No. 6 Western Command: Stourport-on-Severn, Nr Kidderminster, Worcestershire. This college was housed in a former American general hospital.

Overseas there were three main AFC centres:

- ◆ Germany: the College of the (British) Rhine Army at Goettingham.
- ◆ Central Mediterranean Forces: with colleges at Perugia in Italy and Spittal, in Austria.
- ◆ Middle East Land Forces: HQ in Cairo with branches at Alexandra, Mt Carmel and Sarafand (Palestine). These centres were housed in a variety of barracks and aircraft hangars. When the first ATS officer had been appointed at the War Office to examine education facilities in the service it was the view that locally recruited Palestinian members of the ATS were more enthusiastic about any educational facilities that were offered to them than their home-based counterparts.

Gina's Story

ATS member Gina Shadrack has happy memories of Foundation College No. 3 at Chiseldon near Swindon. Her initial experiences as a recruit were not so different from those of many other girls. Gina had lived all her life in Chelmsford in Essex and was sent to Warrington in the north-west for basic training. Her parents were horrified as it seemed so far away and Gina found it very strange to be suddenly living amongst so many other girls. Gina admits to being so homesick that she was almost sent home.

However, she overcame it enough to survive the rough and tumble of a recruit's life and was posted to the staff college at Bagshot Park as a clerk. Bagshot Park was not a requisitioned ancestral home – it had always been a Crown property. Gina remembers helping prepare for the many secret meetings and conferences that were held there, ensuring that a continual supply of papers and pencils is a particular memory.

Then she was posted to Chiseldon. This camp had a varied history, which repeated itself in an educational sense. At the end of the First World War the Ministry of Labour had used it to train unemployed ex-servicemen. It was used for combat training during the Second World War; it provided a collection point for troops returning after the evacuation of Dunkirk; then the Americans and Canadians arrived and an American hospital was established, which took casualties from the D-Day landings. When the camp and hospital were scaled down after May 1945, and the AFC arrived, German and Italian POWs remained to do gardening and cleaning. Gina, and the other ATS girls stationed there, 'knew' some of the prisoners who came to clean the offices, although the absolute rule was 'No Fraternisation'. The men would craft small gifts out of whatever material they could find and leave them in wastepaper baskets in exchange for cigarettes that were left for them. Gina found her time at Chiseldon a great experience because of the variety of courses that were held there for pre-release men and women. If there was ever a space on a course the ATS permanent staff could take advantage of it to learn a new skill. Gina always knew what was going on because, as a clerk, she made all the administrative arrangements for the courses, including booking in the attendees.

She then went off to the ATS OCTU at the Imperial Services College at Windsor. As an officer Gina served at COD Donnington in an administrative capacity, looking after the ATS girls who worked in the depot; her final administrative job was at Hounslow.

Films and Filming

If you talk about films and the ATS in the same breath, somebody will mention *The Gentle Sex*. This film was co-directed and narrated by Leslie Howard, the well-known film star who was later killed when the passenger plane he was on was shot down by the Luftwaffe over the Bay of Biscay. Those taking part in the film included Joan Greenwood, Rosamund John, John Laurie and Miles Malleson.

The language seems rather stilted today, but it was typical of the period in which it was shot. It followed the lives of seven ATS recruits through basic training, trade training and their eventual duties. Designed in part as a recruiting project and partly as entertainment, it was premiered at the Odeon in Leicester Square in 1943. It certainly caught some aspects of ATS life that have been recounted in this book: how girls from different backgrounds formed a bond; how there was always somebody who wasn't popular and was teased about their manner; the difficulties of driving in a convoy and how important vehicle maintenance was; what went on at dances; the challenge of being an Ack-Ack girl.

This was not the only way the ATS was involved in the film world – Pinewood Studies were requisitioned by the War Office for use by the Crown Film Unit and the Army (and RAF) Film and Photographic Unit. The studios had been built in 1936 and in 1939 and J. Arthur Rank became their chairman. The studios were home to a wide range of information and training films that were shown in units, in any available building, and in static or mobile camp cinemas. A few ATS members trained as cinema projectionists, which was a recognised trade in the service. They learnt to operate and maintain the equipment which took 16mm film – this was the standard used by the military at that time. They then visited ATS units to show training films. Others who were posted to Pinewood worked on the film sets where they might become a continuity girl. This is a very important role in film-making but ATS girls were seldom mentioned when the then short list of credits rolled.

There was another activity in the film world – the Army Kinema Section (AKS). Joan Awbery (née Stittle) worked with this service, which had been set up to provide the army with entertainment, particularly on location. She had been posted to Eastern Command on clerical and secretarial duties with the AKS. Although the section was concerned with film it wasn't very glamorous. Those who worked in the ATS company at Wembley, the AKS HQ, remember seeing actors around the place – Richard Greene, Trevor Howard, Jack Hawkins – but, like their ATS colleagues out in Cambridge, they were involved mainly in the routing of mobile cinemas. From Eastern Command HQ in Cambridge AKS projectors were routed round the isolated gun sites, searchlight units and various military camps on the East Anglian coast that weren't static or large enough to have a cinema.

Joan relates her experiences:

For 18 months I was a shorthand typist in the No 3 AKS office housed in the attic of a tall house overlooking Parker's Piece in Cambridge. Four of us in the office and half a dozen operators (only one ATS). They were sent out in Tilley trucks, sometimes for a week at a time, with projectors, screens and cans of film. The crew was warmly welcomed by the isolated soldiers. Films were shown in whatever hut tent or shed was available. More often than not the film broke down to catcalls and stomping of feet. At the end of the run the films came back to us to be rewound and allocated to the next run. It was important to keep track of who had seen what, otherwise there would be complaints. Films we had available included *The Way to the Stars*; *In Which We Serve*; *The Cruel Sea*; *Casablanca*; *Blithe Spirit*; *Warsaw Concerto*.

We had to accept an awful lot of B films from HQ which would get the thumbs-down from our customers although they were probably grateful for anything.

The Army Physical Training Corps

The motto of the APTC goes a long way in explaining its purpose:

mens sana in corpore san
(a healthy mind in a healthy body)

The British Army first realised that its troops didn't have such healthy bodies during the wars and campaigns of the nineteenth century. Thereafter sports and gymnastics were taken very seriously in the army and in 1940 corps status was awarded to the then Army Physical Training Staff, making it the Army Physical Training Corps (APTC).

The ATS was drawn into the requirement for military personnel to do regular PT exercises wherever possible, and usually first thing in the morning. It was always a bone of contention that ATS units who worked in a twenty-four-hour shift system were excused, for example those at the Home Postal Centre or those in mixed batteries of the RA.

An ATS girl would be selected from her unit to attend a three-week training course at the physical training school in Aldershot; courses were run frequently with between twenty and thirty girls on each intake. The girls then returned to their units and made themselves unpopular by getting their colleagues out of bed earlier than was needed for work in order to stretch their bodies and, hopefully, their minds.

It was all explained in one of the standard War Office instruction pamphlets entitled 'Physical and Recreational Training in the ATS 1945'.

Designed for PTIs, it set out quite clearly the purpose of PT and certainly demonstrated the importance of detail:

> The aim of physical education in the ATS is to increase and maintain a standard of physical well-being, and through improving the health of the individual to make it possible for her to use her mental powers to the fullest capacity.

The pamphlet went on to cover teaching methods, preparation of classes, record keeping, rules of all the games that the ATS played, organising cross-country runs, dancing and three pages on skipping. There were suggestions about what to include for sports days, but with a very stern warning that on no account were the ATS girls to take part in a tug-of-war or to compete in any event against men. Was that because they might have beaten them?

Enthusiastic PT Instructors

One ATS lady who wouldn't have been in any danger of overexerting herself during PT sessions was Audrey Williamson, who was a silver medal winner in the London Olympics of 1948. Due to the war these were the first Games to be held since 1936 when the chosen city had been Berlin.

Audrey had joined the ATS in 1944 just after her eighteenth birthday. After basic training she was sent on a PT course then posted to HQ South Midland District in Oxford as a full-time corporal PTI. By the following year she was competing in military athletics competitions at all levels, as she said, 'To set an example as a PTI and to encourage other girls to enter the District meeting'.

It was through her success in service events that she was spotted by the Women's Amateur Athletic Association. By the end of 1947 Audrey, by then Supervising Officer PTI/ATS at HQ North Midland District, was selected as an 'Olympic Possible'.

She attended the ATS OCTU at the Imperial Services College, Windsor, and then went to HQ Western Command, Chester, as Staff Officer PTI/ATS.

Training for the Games began in earnest, although it still had to be fitted around normal duties. Fortunately Audrey's training ground – the Chester Racecourse – was situated just below the officers' mess, which was very convenient for early morning runs. Just before the Games she went for more intensive training to the Army School of Physical Training (ASPT) in Aldershot, which had excellent facilities and dedicated trainers – Audrey's was Captain Harry Harbin APTC who was also an Olympic official.

Eventually Audrey was selected to compete in the 200m sprint and the 400m relay. It was the 200m which drew public attention. In this event she was competing against a well-known Dutch sprinter – Fanny Blankers-Koen, nick-named 'The Flying Housewife'. By the time of the London competition Fanny already held six world records; this was thought to be a great achievement, not least because she had suffered from the same malnutrition that her Dutch compatriots had experienced under Nazi occupation and which had shocked ATS members who served in the area after D-Day. Interestingly, Audrey was very conscious of the importance of diet during training; even during wartime and post-war rationing and shortages, however, she wouldn't have experienced similar malnutrition. At the ASPT she received additional rations and milk, and during the period of the Games extra food was provided; although, in general, all facilities and services were very basic.

During that 200m final Audrey remembered Harry's advice to keep back a reserve of energy for the final push – which took her from fifth place to the silver medal, 0.1 of a second ahead of her nearest rival but 0.7 behind Fanny Blankers-Koen. It was a proud day for her, and the ATS, when she stood on the rostrum to receive her medal.

Audrey died on 29 April 2010.

Beryl Manthorp was another keen exponent of PT. In civilian life she had been involved in all aspects of exercise as a ballet teacher, running her own school of dance. This is a role that she has continued throughout her life.

When it came to wartime enrolment she had one obvious and important question to ask at the recruiting office. The answer was that the WRENS had no history of PT, the WAAF a little and the ATS a lot, and so Beryl became an ATS PTI.

She remembers the 1941 War Office instruction stating that all ATS women were to have daily PT based on the Swedish method.

Beryl explains the organisation of her specialty. Large units had full-time instructors with the rank of corporal. Smaller units had part-time PTIs who could be from any branch of the service and hold any rank. These were supervised on a regular basis by a full-time regional sergeant instructor.

Beryl went to Oswestry anti-aircraft training centre; she served as the regimental PT sergeant with two operational regiments and that took her all over the country supervising PT on gun sites.

When the Anti-Aircraft Command was disbanded at the end of the war Beryl went to ATS PT HQ at Nottingham – one of a team of five with two junior commanders and three sergeants. They covered Nottingham, Derby, Leicester and Chilwell. Beryl was billeted with the Pay Corps in Nottingham and worked mainly with the HPC.

In 1945 PTIs started working with the RAMC on remedial courses, whilst Beryl was still in charge of PT at the ordnance depot in Derby. Her last posting was to Glen Parva Barracks in Leicester, supervising PT training for ATS recruits at the training centre and the OCTU.

Keeping the Records Straight

Joan Halliwell (née Moon) was a record office clerk. After basic training at Talavera Camp in Northampton Joan was posted to the RASC Record Office at the back of Hastings. The office was housed in a stone-built former monastery built on a hill overlooking the town. Joan wasn't with the only ATS unit in Hastings – the Ack-Ack girls were there as well because of the bombing raids and doodlebugs that Joan remembers well.

The Record Office employed 500 ATS girls – B Company and D Company were billeted in large houses nearby. Joan's work involved communications about personnel in the Middle East.

Mary Churchill came to one of the Saturday night dances while her battery was stationed on the Hastings cliff top.

There was an ATS casualty here, unconnected with bombing raids, etc. Private Gladys Field had climbed on to her billet roof to watch the gun flashes across the Channel, but fell to her death. She was twenty-two years old and is buried in Hastings cemetery.

Joan met her future husband when he was serving in a nearby camp. The wedding took place locally with, as Joan says, 'Many khaki-clad guests!'

Cooking with the Army Catering Corps

In the 1930s the government investigated the living standards of the British Army and quickly moved from generalities to the specific subject of catering, which had attracted much criticism. They took advice about rations, food supply, nutrition, training of cooks and the setting of overall higher standards. As a result of these inquiries a new School of Army Cookery was built at the end of the decade at St Omer Barracks in Aldershot. In 1941 the Army Catering Corps (ACC) was formed, with its base also at St Omer Barracks. The ACC came under the jurisdiction of the RASC (until 1965).

In 1941 ATS cooks were attached to, and trained by, the newly formed ACC. Of course it wasn't simply a matter of learning to cook; it was learning to cook for three members of an officers' mess, or twenty senior NCOs in their mess, or thousands of soldiers spread amongst several cookhouses on a large army depot or camp. They also learnt to cook in mobile kitchens and to construct and use field kitchens.

The food providers and cooks in all army units and camps in the Second World War were not the first to be faced with problems of food quantities and supply. In 1704 the Duke of Marlborough worried about an adequate supply of bread for his troops at the Battle of Blenheim; just over a century later the Duke of Wellington also had bread on his mind in relation to the fitness and morale of his troops in Portugal.

They would have welcomed the ATS girls, who were well known for their skills as bakers. There was a static bakery next to the Army School of Cookery where hundreds of auxiliaries were trained and which produced thousands of loaves every day to supply surrounding units.

A senior commander was in overall charge of the ATS girls at the school, with over 300 of all ranks undergoing training at any one time. They qualified as messing officers, sergeant supervisors of ATS cookhouses and instructors for the small ATS cookery schools around the country that carried out basic training of cooks.

Somebody who knew all about the Army School of Cookery was Molly Choppen (née Cooke). As so often happened, it all came about by chance. After basic training Molly wanted to join the ATS Provost and was told that she first had to complete six months of general duties with the ATS before specialising. She was sent to the Army School of Cookery – and didn't leave until she was demobbed.

Molly started off in the company office on clerical duties; then she was encouraged to go on some of the many courses held at the school, learning about subjects as wide-ranging as wine and accounting. Eventually she became the sergeant in charge of the St Omer officers' mess, where there were fifty-six male officers and one ATS officer.

That one ATS officer was well known in the service, not least because she had come from New Zealand, where she had been a Domestic Science teacher. Ethel Keys-Wells had actually come on holiday, intending to travel around Britain and Europe; events interfered with her plans and she enrolled in the ATS the day after war was declared, joining the 1st City of London Company. After being commissioned at Sandhurst, she joined the ACC as a junior commander and instructor at the school, where she served until 1947. She was presented with the MBE (Military) by King George VI in 1946.

Both Molly and Ethel remembered the inspection visit made by Queen Elizabeth and the Princess Royal in 1944.

Junior Commander Ethel Keys-Wells, Army School of Cookery. Courtesy of M. Choppen.

Inspection by HRH Queen Elizabeth (later the Queen Mother) on promenade outside ATS billets in Douglas, Isle of Man. Her daughter, Princess Elizabeth (now Queen Elizabeth II) served with the ATS. Courtesy of M. Moss.

The end of the war didn't see the end of 'ATS catering', however. Ethel Keys-Wells took over and ran a hotel in Cambridge and asked Molly to go and help her in reception and administration; when they advertised for a head cook they had no hesitation in selecting an ACC-trained ATS cook who had, by chance, applied for the job.

There's no record of how many ex-ATS ended up being employed in the hotel. Perhaps three was the limit, but it does highlight one interesting turn of events. Those girls in khaki who were often described, rather snootily, as being 'only cooks' were some of the best qualified to work in civilian life post-war. Many specialised in confectionary, running their own cafes or small shops; others worked, at various management levels, in hotels and leisure facilities like the holiday camps which had been de-requisitioned and returned to operators like Butlins.

Medical Matters

Units would have medical orderlies on their establishment, or medics as they were known. Whether male or ATS, they would not be trained nurses but would be responsible for the smooth running of a medical centre – checking supplies, rolling bandages, emptying bedpans, checking medication, making sure that troops attended for medical checks. Barbara Hudson became an ATS medic attached to an RA regiment in Tulse Hill for part of her service. Such experiences led her to become a qualified nurse in later life.

There was a lot of medical activity around the south-west region of Bristol and Bath. One particular activity that centred on Bristol was the Army Blood Transfusion Service. It was based at Southmead Hospital, with a blood supply depot at Chilton Polden, near Bridgwater in Somerset. ATS girls worked as medical technicians at Southmead. They inspected plasma supplies before they were stored at the army's central blood bank; they packed kits for overseas and blood supplies that went in refrigerated vans. Just another example of the extremely varied tasks that 'girls in khaki' embraced.

Ten

On Location Overseas

Virtually as soon as war broke out, 300 ATS recruits were posted overseas when the British Expeditionary Force was sent to France. This was encouraged by Helen Gwynne-Vaughan, for whom service in France was familiar ground following her time there during the First World War. Towards the end of 1939 she had visited France to establish how the ATS could best meet requirements. In her personal account of her experiences (*Service with the Army*) she tells of her visit to the headquarters of the Lines of Communication at Le Mans.

This expression, usually abbreviated to LOC, occurs constantly when describing the war in Western Europe, in all circumstances, including the accounts of ATS activities. LOC refers to the system used to move the British Army in a structured and methodical way from the ports up through France and Belgium to within about 30 miles of the fighting troops. This meant moving stores, spare parts, non-perishable food, ammunition, replacement clothing, replacement equipment and vehicles, stationery and blood supplies up to the front line on pre-determined routes; as far as was possible under such difficult circumstances the different consignments were kept separate as they would be off-loaded into specific depots when they reached their destination.

One vital part of the LOC was the signal capacity and literally two-way communications carried out by line/cables not radio – as the Germans had the means to de-code some English radio messages. As the signals operations became established and more military lines were introduced, operators were needed who could switch calls between military offices – in addition to the continuing use of dedicated teleprinters. Also needed were switchboard operators and drivers, plus all the support staff that were required for catering, clerical duties and stores control.

Helen Gwynne-Vaughan succeeded in her mission of allocating ATS to the war effort in France; unfortunately, no sooner had several hundred members started work in various locations than Germany pushed through the Allied lines and the British Army was evacuated via Dunkirk. The story is often told of how the group of bilingual ATS telephonists working in Paris were amongst the last British troops to leave France – having dashed out of Paris in a waiting lorry just as the Germans were entering the city from the other side.

Hundreds of ATS also served in the Middle East in areas including Cairo, Alexandria and Tel-el-Kebir. Sarafand in Palestine was a huge camp which had been established in peacetime and now included an ATS training centre for locally recruited ATS members. Many of these Palestinian girls worked in RAOC depots.

The longest serving senior officer in the Middle East was Controller (Colonel) Audrey Chitty. In 1943, as senior commander (major), she was responsible for over 5,000 women; a difficult task involving cultural and language issues and problems over dress codes. In that year she was awarded an OBE (Military). She travelled extensively around the area and attended recruiting parades.

Jessie Gellatly, who had joined the ATS in the winter of 1944, also had problems during her time in the Middle East, albeit at a very junior level and involving insects. After basic training in Dalkeith, where her main achievement, thanks to a bilingual sergeant instructor, was learning to sing *Lili Marlene* in German, she volunteered for overseas service and was sent to the Middle East. She toured around Alexandria, Cairo, Jerusalem and El Adem (a small landing strip in the Western Desert). Her job was to record on disc the voices of service men and women. A shame that such an interesting job was overtaken by misfortune. As Jessie says, 'I think I was bitten by every insect in Egypt and, after scratching, ended up with a skin infection on my legs and was hospitalised in Cairo. Had a gyppy tummy, but who didn't!'

By 1946 the long conflict between Jews and Arabs, based on grievances resulting from the British Mandate in Palestine (due to end in 1948), escalated to a level that caused enormous problems for the British Army.

No. 1 War Office
Holding Unit, ATS at
Ashley Down, Bristol.
Courtesy of J. Awbery.

In early 1947 all British Army families were evacuated to the camp at Sarafand, ahead of their return home. Troop numbers slowly declined. A contingent remained in Allenby Barracks in Jerusalem, surrounded by protective barbed wire; a small group of ATS clerical staff and telephonists also remained behind, billeted in flats vacated by British families and escorted to work in HQ Palestine. They left later in 1947 and the remaining British soldiers in May 1948.

After D-Day, many ATS auxiliaries volunteered for overseas postings. The above illustration might bring back some memories for auxiliaries in transit for Europe. It is Muller's No. 5 Orphanage at Ashley Down, Bristol, which was taken over in 1944 to become the No. 1 War Office Holding Unit ATS.

Chief Controller Leslie Whateley, as Director ATS, had to deal with a problem that arose in late 1944. The House of Commons voted to make overseas postings compulsory for the ATS. There was a long list of exemptions but that didn't stop the uproar that it caused amongst the general public. The director obtained a precious supply of paper to enable her to send to each member of the ATS an explanation of the situation. One pertinent question that was asked by both civilians and military personnel was why some ATS volunteers for overseas service hadn't been sent out. The DATS explained that this was because the trades and qualifications of some volunteers were not those needed by overseas units. A second concern was that the public could see 'fit' male soldiers still in Britain, and wanted to know why they couldn't be sent instead. The Director explained that healthy soldiers were still needed at home. She gave an example in her letter – 'You cannot use a weakling as a Battle School instructor'. Other men might seem fine, but be classed as medically unfit for active service, having been injured. ATS clerks, for example, could find themselves alongside such men. Some might be on embarkation leave waiting to be shipped to the Far East where the war still raged; or they could have just been granted a short spell of home leave to see their family after having been away for five or six years. The DATS was, in effect, reassuring her ATS members about 'compulsion' and suggesting a response that they might make if anyone raised this matter with them. Of course, her message included praise and encouragement:

> Do you realise what a magnificent contribution you have made and are making to the war effort and how much you have helped to build up the name the ATS has now earned? … I have implicit faith in you all and know you will not fail in the last lap of the race.

In November 2010 *The Daily Telegraph* published a detailed obituary of Margot Cooper (née Marshall) who had died on 21 November 2010. Headlined as the first woman officer to set foot in occupied Europe after D-Day, she was also an ATS subaltern. At the beginning of June 1944 she had joined a secret D-Day meeting where General Montgomery outlined his plans for the imminent landings. Margot Marshall was to be in charge of the 1st Continental Group ATS. The group consisted of ATS drivers and shorthand typists, with a couple of Redcaps (military police) – all part of Montgomery's Rear Section of the 21st Army Group. They crossed over to France or, to be precise, to the beach at Courseulles, landing on an LST (Landing Ship Tank) with their vehicles whose waterproofing for the beach landing might well have been done by their ATS colleagues in an ordnance depot. Courseulles was a less familiar name associated with the landing of supplies on the Normandy coast after D-Day. It was one of three smaller ports – the others being Isigny and Port-en-Bessin – used for this purpose. The Allies also relied on the Mulberry Harbour at Arromanches or delivered supplies over open beaches such as Utah, these latter two locations having links to our ATS story.

The 1st Continental Group was then expanded to include three companies of cooks, drivers and clerks who arrived a few weeks later. The whole camp was set up around Bayeux, where the British Army established their main supply dumps during the battle for Normandy. Then, in September 1944, it moved to Brussels where the troops received a heroes' welcome. *The Daily Telegraph* obituary reports that:

> In the spring of 1945 senior Allied and Nazi officers met to address the worsening problem of food shortages in the Northern Netherlands. A temporary truce was

agreed and subsequently Margot Marshall was posted to 3rd Continental Group ATS, Netherlands District, as Junior Commander. She formed K Company to secure food supplies for the starving Dutch people.

The problem of food shortages in the Netherlands had been exacerbated by the failure of the Allied armies to push forward and cross the Rhine, thus defeating the Germans there in late 1944. This, it is argued, would have allowed them to transport some food supplies into Holland. For readers who are not happy with that briefest of brief descriptions of an enormously complex subject, military historian Robin Neilland's *The Battle for the Rhine 1944. Arnhem and the Ardennes: the Campaign in Europe* is a fascinating account of the Rhine issue.

As if she hadn't had enough challenges, Margot Marshall was then ordered to form a temporary ATS company to look after the British delegation at the Potsdam Conference. In July and August 1945 US, British and Soviet Union leaders – Truman, Churchill and Stalin – met at Potsdam (about 18 miles south-west of Berlin) to discuss the post-war administration of Germany. Potsdam was considered to be the home of Prussian militarism and the main conference was held in a former palace of the Prussian royal family. Surrounding villas were requisitioned for the hundreds of officials who accompanied the heads of state. To handle the requirements of the

British section of this vast gathering, Margot selected about 140 ATS girls and they flew to Berlin for five weeks. She and her colleagues were invited to the Berlin Victory Parade where they had a box next to Churchill's.

Junior Commander Marshall was then demobbed in April 1946 and married Major John Cooper. An impressive overseas wartime career for this ATS officer, worthy of the media reporting.

Lance-Corporal M.M. Collinson (later Pidgeon) at Bad Oeynhausen, April 1946. Courtesy of M. Pidgeon.

Still, to Lance Corporal Merville Collinson (now Merville Pidgeon) she was just 'Miss Marshall'. Merville herself had an interesting ATS career and seemed to be constantly on the move. She was one of the many hundreds of ATS who volunteered for overseas service after D-Day. She left on 18 August 1944 and followed in Miss Marshall's footsteps thereafter. Her story, which started at Guildford in 1942, is told below in her own words:

During October 1942 I received my marching orders to report to Guildford Camp, where I received training for three weeks or so. In fact I was there when I reached my 21st birthday; I was given a days leave and on my return was given a surprise party and cake from the very kind members I had only recently met. A very nice beginning to four years of a completely different world. (Merville was selected to do typing and secretarial work.)

I was posted to Norfolk with 601 H.A.A. (M) Battery. It was a bitterly cold winter and when we left for Northern Ireland a few months later, I was able to make a perfect Union Jack in the snow with my red and blue ink pots!

We were stationed just outside Belfast at Greencastle and I shared a Nissen hut with several other girls. We had a rounded coal fire to keep warm – which was probably not a good health idea – but we all got on very well together.

I worked in the HQ office but during my time there attended a Physical Training (PT) course so, on my return, made myself probably very unpopular by taking the rest of the BHQ for early morning exercises!

The first OC (Officer Commanding) we had was a Major Higgens who did not like women in the Army so, whenever we organised a game of hockey, or suchlike, he would take every opportunity to hit our ankles!! Apart from this he was quite human and pleasantly polite to us.

The HQ team took their turn in manning the searchlight and the German planes did bomb Belfast so we all had to be on the alert. Later we returned to England and, in particular, Gosport where we saw more bombing.

During my time there I volunteered for Overseas duty and found myself joining the 21st Army Group and on the 12th August 1944 we landed at Caen, where we lived under tents and also worked in tents – I often wonder which field I worked and lived in on my yearly return to Normandy – with the New Forest Normandy Veterans.

The troops pushed ahead and in September we arrived in Brussels where the people were still cheering the troops – and us! – we, my friend and I, were approached by a young woman who invited us back to her house to meet her mother. Her brother was in a concentration camp as he was a Communist. We visited them regularly and were always made most welcome. We also met a young couple who regularly invited us to their home. We enjoyed a wonderful Christmas party there, plenty of food – a huge plate of oysters – and lots of presents. They ran a bookshop and were always so charming and generous.

We regularly visited the Monty Club and enjoyed many tea dances – as there were so few British dancers there we were always lucky in getting the really good dancers to dance with!

Early in 1945 my friend, Mary, and I were seconded to the Netherlands District HQ. Our accommodation was with two sisters in Tilburg. They were lovely and looked after us so well – they made lovely icecream and completely spoilt us!

We were then sent to Utrecht where we stayed with an elderly couple – well, actually they were probably middle-aged! – they could not speak English – and we could not speak Dutch, so it was a little difficult. However, when I received a food parcel from my Mother, despite the fact that she probably had less rations than we had – there was a tin of coffee and when I gave this and some of the other things to the woman, she threw her arms round me and gave me a big kiss! Coffee was gold dust, but we had all the food we needed. We knew that some of the soldiers were dealing in the black market, especially with their cigarettes, but I thought this was despicable when the people we were freeing from tyranny had so little.

Our next port of call was The Hague where we lived in Army Barracks. Each day after our meal and when the leftover food (from our plates) was collected a long queue of local people arrived to take what they could. It was heartbreaking. I even saw an old woman pick up something from the street and eat it.

The starving people in The Hague have always left an indelible mark in my memory, also for their stoicism and quiet acceptance of what must have been a very painful experience.

Two happy memories remain; the first when Major Brabner and Captain Day took me to hear Princess Juliana speak and the second was being given a lift in Queen Wilhelmina's car in The Hague, her chauffeur spoke perfect English! When I told Major Brabner about this adventure the next day, he asked if I ever read anything I typed as hitching lifts was forbidden!!

The Netherlands District HQ badge was a blue windmill on a white background, but I have never seen any acknowledgement of this on any wartime chart of badges.

At this time I was typing reports from the concentration camps and the statistics were horrific. None of this sunk in at the time. We also heard of the awful things happening at the time in Brussels to the collaborators. The Dutch Nazis were also still around and we were warned to be careful when we left the camp.

The Montgomery Club, Brussels. . Courtesy of M. Pidgeon.

One day we were interviewed by Miss Marshall who was recruiting ATS to help at Potsdam. We were told that secretaries were not required (the politicians had their own secretaries) and we would be expected to do light duties only, but as the historic event was so great it was thought that we should be included in such a great event. We accepted straightaway.

At Potsdam we were billeted in a lovely old house and were very comfortable. We were sent to Churchill's house the first morning and asked by his valet to make the great man's bed, also, that he liked to have his sheets changed every day. Fair enough, but on leaving we were told to return that evening as there was to be a great banquet and there would be lots of washing up to do! I quickly said that we were not there to wash up after a banquet as I did not think that this was a 'light duty'. The valet drew himself up to his full height and said most royally 'You should consider it a great honour to wash up for Mr Churchill'. So we went to Miss Marshall to tell her the sorry story. She was very understanding and told us to report to Lord Portel's office the next day.

Merville Collinson with friends (Mary, Vicky, ?), The Hague, 1945. Courtesy of M. Pidgeon.

This was a doddle. All we did was to make the mid-morning coffee and the afternoon tea. The Marines came in twice a day to bring delicious cakes too. There was also a swimming pool there. So we had a really good time but I often wonder who did all the washing up!

After Potsdam we returned to 21st Army Group Headquarters at Bad Oeynhausen, there we played lots of hockey and netball against the men.

Another pleasant memory was seeing the Victory Parade in Berlin on 21st July and Messrs. Churchill, Anthony Eden, Clement Atlee, Field Marshall Alexander, Field Marshall Montgomery and the Russian and American soldiers also in the Parade.

Merville (Lance Corporal Collinson) was Mentioned in Dispatches for her work in the Netherlands.

Unexpected Duties

Annie Smart (née Chalmers) had served in Antwerp with a HAA mixed battery of the RA. When the war ended she was posted to Brussels where, always paired off with another ATS girl, they patrolled the streets looking out for girls in khaki who were not wearing their uniform according to regulations or were misbehaving in some way. Annie found that rather boring, so she applied to go on a Military Police (MP) course with 110 Provost Company in Paderborn, Germany.

The Corps of Military Police (CMP) had expanded rapidly after the start of the war and by 1943 it had 32,000 members, including an ATS Provost Section which had been formed in 1942. The CMP served in all areas, all war zones and all countries where there were British troops. (Its royal prefix was awarded by the king in 1946 in recognition of its wartime service.)

The course was fairly routine, covering all aspects of military law and how the corps handled the various problems that its police had to deal with. The only thing that Annie thought was a bit different was that they were taught self-defence. Off she went with other ATS colleagues expecting to be put on duties relating to miscreant ATS girls.

Not quite! She found herself at No. 5 Civilian Internment Camp Sennelager, Germany, in charge of Nazi SS female guards from Ravensbrucke concentration camp, awaiting their summons to the war crimes trial in Hamburg in 1946.

During the day she guarded the prisoners while they were carrying out various jobs like cleaning. At night the ATS Provost went out with both German and British Military Police to find and arrest SS women who'd been identified but not yet caught. Annie reckoned that, when the police had discovered where they were hiding, the trick was to catch them after they'd gone to bed and take them by surprise before they could escape. The ATS taught its members a wide range of skills!

Historic Duties

Susan Hibbert (née Heald) had a curious connection with the ATS during her early life. She was educated at the Godolphin School in Salisbury which became a billet for the ATS during the war; so she shares slightly different memories of the same building with Betty Mitchell, who served at the Southern Command Pay Office in Salisbury and whose story was told earlier.

Susan had been to secretarial college and could speak French so that, after joining the ATS and completing her basic training, she was entrusted with work that involved classified documents before being posted to General Eisenhower's HQ in London. She then moved to the Supreme Headquarters Allied Expeditionary Force (SHAEF) in Reims, France.

Subsequently, as a staff sergeant secretary with SHAEF, she found herself typing the English version of the German surrender document, while others typed the French, Russian and German versions. It took a week of drafting and re-drafting. Susan was Mentioned in Dispatches for her work with General Eisenhower.

Susan Hibbert died in 2009 but, as her obituary in *The Daily Telegraph* reported, she completed one further historic task associated with the German surrender. She signalled the War Office in London with the first notification of the surrender – 'The mission of this Allied Force was fulfilled at 0241, local time, May 7th 1945'.

Between Here and There

Another group of ATS girls who served overseas (just) were remembered with gratitude. They ran the No. 3 Port Staging Camp at Calais.

The camp operated between November 1945 and June 1947, providing overnight accommodation for troops and civilians returning home, either on leave or permanently. They might have been happy to arrive in Calais, but they were also tired and hungry, having made long, uncomfortable journeys.

The girls of No. 3 Camp kept an informal visitors book for 'guests' who wanted to make comments. A good idea as the whole book was one long list of thanks – for the hospitality, the welcoming service, the food and, of course, the hot baths.

Staff of No. 3 ATS Port Staging Camp at Calais, plus some additional doggy helpers! Courtesy of the National Army Museum.

Eleven

The ATS and Society

The ATS was restructured into the Women's Royal Army Corps (WRAC) in February 1949. Their service during the Second World War had been much appreciated, vital in many areas and a demonstration of just how much women could achieve when given the opportunity.

It may be tempting to compare the experiences of those serving in the ATS with the lives of women today. It's hardly informative or relevant, however, to slot ATS recollections into the current social framework of sex, gender issues, glass ceilings and equality. Such a temptation should be resisted in favour of looking at the ATS in the context of its own framework when analysing the achievements of the women in khaki, i.e. the structure of society in the first half of the last century and that of a country at war.

The social background that surrounded the ATS as it was established and expanded was that of a rigid class structure and its accompanying divisions and snobbery. Many in one half of society really didn't know how the other half lived, especially if the two halves were also subject to the North/South divide. It would have taken a lot of sensitive understanding to picture the cities from which some recruits had come with nits in their hair. Conversely, recruits from 'average' working-class homes disliked the patronising attitude and grating accents of the early officers who had been mistakenly recruited according to the criteria of their place on a county's social ladder.

It brings to mind the old adage that 'if you want to explore a person's character don't look at how they treat their peers and seniors; look at how they behave towards those over whom they have authority or seniority.' Those who have served in uniform will have their own interpretations of that advice.

It says a lot for the value of a standard uniform and common experiences in difficult times that the majority of ATS recruits who shared huts and hardships throughout basic and further training bonded well; some became friends for life.

Reputation

The attitude of the public in general to the ATS girls was rather strange. There was a view, encouraged in the early years for some reason by the Beaverbrook Press (a collection of newspapers and journals that included the *Daily Express*), that the ATS was the worst option for women who wanted to join the women's services and their papers criticised the girls in khaki whenever they saw an opportunity, especially if they could talk about morals and promiscuity. One theory is that Lord Beaverbrook, who was Minister of Aircraft Production in 1940 and 1941 (and Minister of Supply and of War Production subsequently), thought that it was a waste of effort for women to join the forces and play at being soldiers when they would be more use working on one of his factory production lines!

It's true that factories which were manufacturing war supplies were short of labour, having lost male employees who were eligible for conscription. However, they could attract publicity in a way that was not available to the armed forces. The best-known example of this was Dame Laura Knight's painting of Ruby Loftus, commissioned by the Ministry of Supply. Ruby famously made breech rings for the Bofors gun at the Royal Ordnance Factory in Newport. It was a very skilled and important job, which few could do, and Ruby had been specially selected by the Ministry of Supply. The portrait, which had an element of glamour about it, was hung at the Royal Academy's summer exhibition in 1943 amidst much publicity and declared the Picture of the Year.

Well before this there were reports that when female conscription for women into war work was announced at the end of 1941 some mothers had tried to persuade their daughters to opt for factory work (which for many wasn't going to be quite like that depicted in Dame Laura's painting) rather than join the ATS, with the poor reputation that they'd read or heard about.

An illustration that was, arguably, the ATS equivalent of the Ruby Loftus one was a recruiting poster designed by Abram Games who had started designing posters for the War Office in 1941. The press nicknamed his ATS poster 'The Blonde Bombshell'; Parliament decreed that it was far too glamorous, gave the wrong impression and it was withdrawn.

The ATS recruited from a far wider female population than the WRAF and the WRENS who could, arguably, afford to be more selective. After all, those two services employed fewer women. The WRENS, who were reputed to select their recruits largely through personal recommendation, peaked at approximately 75,000 in 1944. The WAAF peaked at 180,000 in 1943. The ATS peaked at around 220,000, although by the end of the war some 300,000 had actually passed through the service. Correspondingly, in Britain, the army peaked at nearly 3 million men, while the navy had fewer than 800,000 and the RAF peaked at marginally over 1 million.

So perhaps the sheer numbers and range of 'types' in the British Army suggested to mothers that girls would be constantly exposed to temptation and encouraged to give in. Perhaps it was the disorganised and ill-equipped status of the first volunteers that had got their reputation off to a bad start. Some of those volunteers, finding that there wasn't any proper full-time work for them to do, left and would have broadcast critical comments. This was why Dame Helen Gwynne-Vaughan wanted official enrolment with pay, not volunteers, and why her two successors worked so hard on the image problem.

One thing that drew an unfavourable comparison between the ATS and the other two services was the uniform. That dull, drab khaki compared with the smart blues of the WRENS and WAAF – a rather curious reason for disparaging an army of women who were fighting a war! Of course they wore khaki – army uniform was khaki, the First World War QMAAC wore khaki, manufacturing companies on contract to the War Office had warehouses full of khaki serge, and lurking in the background was the Treasury. Uniforms could be produced for the initial estimate of 17,000 girls reasonably quickly, and even so not everyone got all items of kit at the same time. When it was decided that a women's permanent corps would be established as a successor to the ATS in 1949, the idea of a more attractive uniform was obviously on the agenda. It was introduced in 1962–63. That gap was longer than the war and the ATS had existed, so perhaps it was a good idea to clothe the adaptable ATS in their drab khaki before Hitler moved his first Luftwaffe groups and panzer divisions into action.

Pregnancy rates amongst ATS members were probably not a great deal higher than they would have been in the thirties in similar groups of women, but there were now two changes in circumstances. During peacetime, young people lived in small communities, surrounded by family and friends who stayed together throughout their school years. Many were ignorant about sex, let alone contraception, but if a girl became pregnant by a boy from the next street he would usually marry her. For ATS girls, far from home, by the time they realised what had happened to them the man could be long gone overseas to the front line or the other end of the country.

Sexual naivety extended across the social divides, with upper-class girls and debutantes being as ignorant as those from middle or lower-class backgrounds; ATS veterans admit that they had no idea what a lesbian was when they joined.

For couples who intended to get married but where, through naivety or fear of the consequences, the girl didn't want anything more than what was then called 'heavy petting', there was usually no real pressure beyond waiting for the wedding day. However, for an ATS girl the pressure would intensify when her fiancé was on embarkation leave – with the possibility looming over them that he would become a battle casualty and not return.

For a girl who was unmarried, pregnancy meant disapproval and the possibility of being ostracised from family and friends. Added to which the girl would then have to leave the ATS when she was three months' pregnant. The military made no provision for such cases as they then became civilians, yet civilian councils and charities viewed them as an army responsibility.

However, the experiences of ATS veterans shed a different light on how the service was viewed by the public – they remember acts of great kindness from the civilians with whom they came into contact. Many of the girls celebrated their twenty-first birthday while serving and there was often a local lady or cafe owner who would bake a cake or throw a party for them. Some offered them a real luxury like a warm bath. Would such consideration be shown to a women's organisation that was rumoured to be inefficient or promiscuous?

Afterwards

Pre-war male attitudes didn't change completely during the war years and weren't to do so for many years afterwards. Perhaps the distrust or dislike of women within the male preserves of army life arose amongst those who hadn't actually been assisted by the girls in khaki during the threatening years; or amongst those who were anxious about their peacetime jobs which had been done so efficiently by the ATS; or perhaps it had nothing to do with military attitudes. After all it was another two decades before some men started to come to terms with women wearing trousers to work and certain clubs allowed female members to wear trousers in the public rooms only if they were designed as part of a matching two-piece outfit.

When demobilisation (as opposed to victory) came, with the perceived relief and joy that everyone assumed it would bring, it actually proved to be a disturbing event for many. Much has been written about the problems faced by returning military personnel in 1946/47. Alan Allport has written a comprehensive account of post-war difficulties called, simply, Demobbed.

ATS members faced their own difficulties. They had initially been recruited specifically to release male personnel for the front line; so those men expected to come back to take up their old jobs, thereby releasing women 'to return to their home environment and produce babies', as one ATS veteran was told.

Many women left the service willingly; they may have been married during the war and, with their new husbands also due for demob, they wanted to set up their own home together. Although for many that meant living with parents because there was a massive housing shortage in the 1940s. Others were keen to stay on working in uniform, preferably in newly discovered roles.

It was difficult for those who fell between the two ends of the spectrum. ATS members who had served as male replacements were moved around doing all kinds of general work while decisions were made about either their discharge or their suitability for continued service. Due to actual or perceived pressure during this period, combined with uncertainties about the future of the ATS, many women didn't have time to stand still and work out exactly what they wanted to do in the future. This was the feeling that, in large part, gave rise to the later comment: 'I wish I hadn't come out at the end of the war'.

Perhaps the subsequent years of food rationing, clothing coupons and dried egg powder encouraged them to view their ATS years through rose-tinted spectacles, but there is no doubt that ex-ATS girls did have genuine regrets – over leaving their uniforms behind, their positions of authority, their sense of being valued and the close friendships that were and are made during service years. Some of those who had left the service after the war ended actually re-enlisted because they couldn't re-adapt to civilian life with regular working hours or perhaps a lack of regular meals or friends who didn't understand what life had been like in the military and didn't want to talk about it.

The divorce rate rose. Joan Awbery, who was posted as a secretary in Army Legal Services in BAOR for the latter part of her service, found that most of her work involved applications for divorce from soldiers who had been home on leave after several years only to find that their wife had disappeared with someone else or there was a child that couldn't possibly be theirs. Whilst many civilians could often muster some sympathy for single girls who had become pregnant and couldn't marry the father, there was strong disapproval of wives who 'played around' while their husbands were away fighting. ATS members who had married hastily, swept away perhaps by the perceived excitement of a wartime wedding, discovered that the husband who returned to become a civilian wasn't quite as desirable as he had seemed when a soldier in uniform. The ATS girl might have had three or four years, between the marriage and demob, to develop her skills, obtain promotion and build a vision of a better future for herself. However, that's not to forget those wartime marriages that lasted for over sixty years and still continue today.

Whatever the circumstances, the ambitions, the difficulties, it is certain that few ATS members in 1945 or 1946 were the same girls that had joined as raw recruits in earlier times.

Epilogue

As the generations move on young students are in danger of treating the Second World War as just a subject on the history syllabus. A few, very few, are fortunate enough for it to be 'living history' courtesy of elderly relatives. Fewer still, somehow almost with a degree of disbelief, see it through the eyes of relatives who served with the ATS. Betty Mitchell, whose story is told earlier, takes delight in such a generation gap, as displayed in the following verse:

QUESTION AND ANSWER
(With apologies to Lewis Carroll)
'You are old, Auntie Betty,' my great-niece said.
'And your hair has become very white.
Did you really belong in the Army,
Did you really wear khaki and fight?'

'In my youth,' I replied to this curious young lass,
'Young ladies didn't often leave home.
But the war changed all that, and we joined up in droves
We longed for new paths to roam.'

'You are old,' said my niece, 'as I mentioned before.
Can you really remember it all?'
'Oh yes,' I replied, 'I remember the fun,
And the fear – England's back to the wall.'

'We trained for three weeks, that sorted us out,
Doing jobs never tackled before.
We were drilled on the square till we got it just right
After all – WE were fighting this war.'

'Now you're old,' said my niece, 'do you really think
That those years were wasted for you?'
'Oh no,' I replied, 'I learned such a lot –
How to mix, how to cope, to get through.'

'If you're old,' said my niece, 'I cannot suppose
That your nerves are as steady as ever.
Yet you still do things that I cannot do.
What made you so awfully clever?'

'In my youth, when I served, I learned to take charge,
To make full use of my brain.
To decide about payments, to apply Army rules,
Why – I'd do it again and again.'

'Oh well, Auntie Betty, it's all long ago.
I'm glad you remember so well.
When I write up my homework about World War Two
I'll have such a lot I can tell.'

I replied with a smile, 'I wondered just why –
It seemed to me some mystery –
Why you asked all these questions concerning my youth,
Am I part of our land's history?'

Betty Mitchell, Sergeant ATS, 6th Gloucester Clerical Company, Salisbury

The unveiling of the ATS Memorial at the National Memorial Arboretum, 15 July 2006. Courtesy of L. Bowyer.

Sadly, not all the girls in khaki survived to see how their example contributed to the opening up of future opportunities for women who wanted to serve their country. Relatively few died as a result of direct enemy action but hundreds died at home and overseas in accidents and from illness.

The first ATS casualty killed during enemy bombing in England was Private Nora Caveney. She was an Ack-Ack girl who was operating a predictor on a South Coast gun site in April 1942. A bomb fell nearby and Nora was hit by a splinter from it. She had been tracking a German plane and was on target when hit. As she fell another ATS operator took her place and continued with the action.

The worst incident was a bombing raid on an ATS hostel in in Great Yarmouth on 11 May 1943. Twenty-six girls were killed. Six ATS signals operators were commended for 'maintaining army communication throughout the whole day and night, dealing faultlessly with the heavy signals traffic'. In May 1994 Lady Soames (Churchill's daughter and ATS veteran) unveiled a granite plaque in Great Yarmouth in remembrance of the ATS girls who had died in this incident.

Single ATS headstone in Caister cemetery, Great Yarmouth. Courtesy of J. Awbery.

Caister cemetery, Great Yarmouth. Six ATS casualty headstones and two soldiers were also killed at this incident. Courtesy of J. Awbery.

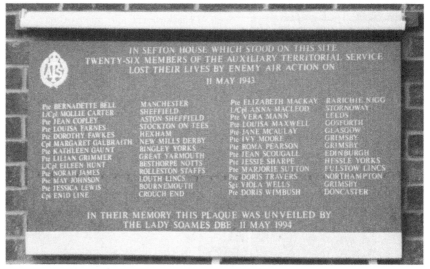

IN SEFTON HOUSE WHICH STOOD ON THIS SITE
TWENTY-SIX MEMBERS OF THE AUXILIARY TERRITORIAL SERVICE
LOST THEIR LIVES BY ENEMY AIR ACTION ON
11 MAY 1943

Pte BERNADETTE BELL	MANCHESTER	Pte ELIZABETH MACKAY	RARICHIE NIGG
L/Cpl MOLLIE CARTER	SHEFFIELD	L/Cpl ANNA MACLEOD	STORNOWAY
Pte JEAN COPLEY	ASTON SHEFFIELD	Pte VERA MANN	LEEDS
Pte LOUISA FARNES	STOCKTON ON TEES	Pte LOUISA MAXWELL	GOSFORTH
Pte DOROTHY FAWKES	HEXHAM	Pte JANE MCAULAY	GLASGOW
Cpl MARGARET GALBRAITH	NEW MILLS DERBY	Pte IVY MOORE	GRIMSBY
Pte KATHLEEN GAUNT	BINGLEY YORKS	Pte ROMA PEARSON	GRIMSBY
Pte LILIAN GRIMMER	GREAT YARMOUTH	Pte JEAN SCOUGALL	EDINBURGH
L/Cpl EILEEN HUNT	BESTHORPE NOTTS	Pte JESSIE SHARPE	HESSLE YORKS
Pte NORAH JAMES	ROLLESTON STAFFS	Pte MARJORIE SUTTON	FULSTOW LINCS
Pte MAY JOHNSON	LOUTH LINCS	Pte DORIS TRAVERS	NORTHAMPTON
Pte JESSICA LEWIS	BOURNEMOUTH	Sgt VIOLA WELLS	GRIMSBY
Cpl ENID LINE	CROUCH END	Pte DORIS WIMBUSH	DONCASTER

IN THEIR MEMORY THIS PLAQUE WAS UNVEILED BY
THE LADY SOAMES DBE 11 MAY 1994

Unveiling of the plaque commemorating the twenty-six ATS members who lost their lives in the enemy air action on 11 May 1943. The standard bearer is Lucy Bowyer. Courtesy of L. Bowyer.

Seventeen girls were lost when a Lancaster aircraft crashed into the sea in bad weather as it flew between RAF Glatton and Pomigliano in Italy in October 1945. It disappeared some 30 miles off the Italian coast. The flight was one of many that operated between Italy and England as part of an operation to bring military personnel (including ATS) home on leave or for discharge and to fly replacements out.

Far from home six ATS girls, serving with 483 (M) HAA Battery/139 Regiment RA in Belgium, died when their troop carrier crashed into a train on a level crossing near Leuven. The girls had been invited to a Coldstream Guards dance. They are buried in the CWGC cemetery at Heverlee in Belgium.

All departed ATS comrades are remembered by friends and colleagues and the younger generations that stretch down through family life. This is especially so on 11 November. However, true remembrance amongst those who have worn uniform doesn't require a poppy; it lives in the heart.

The Collect

This is the Collect of the WRAC Association which incorporates the QMAAC and the ATS:

> O merciful God and Father of us all, whose will is that we should help one another, give to us the grace that we may fulfil the same. Make us gentle, courteous and forbearing. Direct our lives so that we may have courage and resolution in the performance of our duties and hallow all our comradeship by the blessing of thy spirit. For His sake, who loved us and gave himself for us, Jesus Christ our Lord.
> Amen

One ATS headstone in Heverlee cemetery (CWGC). Courtesy of S. Rogers, the War Graves Photographic Project.

Select Bibliography

Banks, Jill M., *Secrets and Soldiers*, The National Trust, 2004

Bidwell, Shelford, *The Women's Royal Army Corps*, Leo Cooper, 1977

Bigland, Eileen, *Britain's Other Army: The Story of the ATS*, Nicholson & Watson, 1946

Britain's Modern Army Illustrated, Odhams Press, 1942

Fernyhough, A.H. Brigadier, CBE MC, *History of the Royal Army Ordnance Corps 1920–1945*, Royal Army Ordnance Corps, 1967

Gwynne-Vaughan, Dame Helen, *Service with the Army*, Hutchinson, 1942

Haslam, Captain M.J., RAOC, 'The Chilwell Story', *RAOC Corps Gazette*, 1982

Lawton, E.R. and Major M.W. Sackett, *The Bicester Military Railway*, Oxford Publishing Company, 1992

Longmate, Norman, *The Doodlebugs: The Story of the Flying Bombs*, Hutchinson, 1981

Pile, General Sir Frederick, GCB DSO MC, 'The Anti-Aircraft Defence of the UK from 28 July 1939 to 15 April 1945', supplement to *The London Gazette*, Tuesday 16 December 1947

Popham, Hugh, *The FANY in Peace & War*, Pen & Sword (rev. edn), 2003

Sherman, Margaret, *No Time for Tears*, George G. Harrap, 1944

Whateley, Dame Leslie, *As Thoughts Survive*, Hutchinson, 1948

Index

Lightning Source UK Ltd.
Milton Keynes UK
UKOW06f0152211015

261041UK00001B/17/P